PENGUIN BOOKS

1001 NAMES FOR AUSTRALIAN BABIES

Suzanne Cater is a
Melbourne freelance writer
and the mother
of two teenage daughters
who are named
Amelia and Elissa.

1001 NAMES FOR AUSTRALIAN BABIES

SUZANNE CATER

PENGUIN BOOKS

Penguin Books Australia Ltd
487 Maroondah Highway, PO Box 257
Ringwood, Victoria, 3134, Australia
Penguin Books Ltd
Harmondsworth, Middlesex, England
Viking Penguin Inc.
40 West 23rd Street, New York, NY 10010, USA
Penguin Books Canada Limited
2801 John Street, Markham, Ontario, Canada, L3R 1B4
Penguin Books (N.Z.) Ltd
182-190 Wairau Road, Auckland 10, New Zealand

First published by Penguin Books Australia, 1989
Reprinted 1990
10 9 8 7 6 5 4 3 2

Copyright © Penguin Books Australia, 1989

All Rights Reserved. Without limiting the rights under copyright
reserved above, no part of this publication may be reproduced,
stored in or introduced into a retrieval system, or transmitted,
in any form or by any means (electronic, mechanical, photocopying,
recording or otherwise), without the prior written permission
of both the copyright owner and the above publisher of this book.

Typeset in Bembo by Leader Composition Pty Ltd
Made and printed in Australia by The Book Printer, Maryborough, Victoria

CIP

Cater, Suzanne, 1947— .
1001 Names for Australian babies.

ISBN 0 14 012190 0.
1. Names, Personal – Australia. I. Title.

929.4'4'0994

INTRODUCTION

Names are gifts which parents choose for children; gifts to last a lifetime and labels which distinguish us from others.

The inspiration for selection has changed through the ages. Names were often chosen with a religious or magical significance. Myths, sagas and legends provided models after whom children were named. The Israelites often incorporated a syllable signifying Jehovah, such as 'iah' which they believed would ensure future happiness.

Many ancient names described personal features or appearance. The girl's name Aithne is derived from a Celtic word meaning 'little fire', and was given to a baby girl with red hair. The Gaelic boy's name Cameron means 'crooked nose'.

'Flower' names were popular in Greece and were

widely used by the Scots. With the current interest in cottage gardens, Daisy, Rose, Poppy, Marigold and Primrose may well become popular again.

The Domesday Book records England's first census in 1086. This survey was ordered by William I who wanted to know the value of his tenants' estates for taxation purposes. Many of the names we use today are recorded in the two volumes of this first listing of early English names. It is from records such as the *Domesday Book* that we have been able to learn the history and meanings of names passed on to us, giving us the opportunity to continue traditions with the names we choose, or to develop new variations on old names.

During the Middle Ages, the Bible and the Saints' calendar were major sources of names, but the Renaissance revived interest in names from the Latin and Greek classics.

The Protestant Reformation of the sixteenth century had a great effect on the popularity of names of Popes. The Puritans further encouraged the use of Old Testament names, and for their girls chose 'virtue' names such as Faith, Hope, Charity, Prudence and Constance.

New names appear every day, many of which are pure invention. Others are new versions of the old. As names pass from country to country and are translated into different languages, many variations of the original exist. The English name John was originally the Hebrew Jochanaan and became Jean in French, Jon or Jones in Welsh, Sean in Irish – along with the variations of Eoghan, Eoin, Seamus, Shamus, Shane and Shawn. The Italian form is Giovanni, Spanish is Juan, German is Hans, Russian is Ivan – and there are many more! Each variation is now as acceptable as John in the changing Australian population.

There is currently a trend for the English names popular in the Victorian era – Victoria, Alexandra, William and Charles. The jewel-loving Edwardians chose names like Ruby, Pearl, Amethyst, and Crystal. Perhaps it is their turn next!

There have always been cycles of fashionable or 'in' names, influenced by royalty, literature, singers and actors. Many parents may now choose Beatrice, following the Duke and Duchess of York.

There are more names for girls than boys; parents are simply more adventurous when it comes to girls' names and are more ready to 'invent' them. Another reason is that there are many feminine versions of the masculine, such as Louise from Louis, or Michelle from Michael. The reverse situation is rare. Gilberta is one of the few feminine/masculine names where the original is the feminine, and the masculine, Gilbert, developed from it.

Many people dislike their given name and would appreciate the chance to change. Those with a second name have that option. Sometimes parents introduce the use of the second name as a first because it sounds better that way. Australia has had three Prime Ministers known by their second given name; Joseph Benedict (Ben) Chifley, Edward Gough Whitlam and John Malcolm Fraser. The senior Whitlams may have felt that Gough Edward Whitlam just didn't sound right!

New names which sound great today may not suit for a lifetime, and while there is no harm in being different, foresight is necessary.

Rhythm and phonetic balance should be considered, but however careful we are in selecting names, Australians can't help themselves inventing nicknames or adding the odd syllable. But parents can avoid unfortunate initials. If the Gibsons choose Penelope Ingrid or David Arthur, their offspring could have an unhappy time when nicknames are bestowed on them at school!

About a quarter of a million babies are born in Australia each year, and the naming of them can involve at least a million parents, grandparents, sisters and brothers! I hope this book can help.

Suzanne Cater
aka Sue, Suzie, Suze, Zannie, Suella, and Mum.

GIRLS

A

Abella: Latin meaning 'the beautiful'. A fine name for every parent's baby girl.

Abigail: 'A father's joy', or 'a source of joy', this Hebrew name became popular in English-speaking countries soon after the Reformation. It became synonymous with 'serving girl' because of Abigail Masham, lady-in-waiting to Queen Anne. Abigail is again a popular name and well accepted above stairs.

Also Abbey, Abbie, Gail, Gale or Gayle.

Abra: A magical name meaning 'mother of multitudes', this is the feminine form of the Hebrew Abraham. In ancient Egypt Abra was a charm word used in incantation, as in abracadabra.

Acacia: A Greek flower name honouring St Acacius, 'the good angel'. It was given to both male and female children of the Christians of Greece and Rome.

Ada: Teutonic, meaning 'prosperous and happy'. A popular girl's name during Victorian times, it is also the accepted diminutive of Adela, Adelaide, Adelina, Adeline.

Adonia: 'Beautiful lady', this feminine form of the Greek Adonis describes the festival of Adonia, celebrated by all Greek women.

Adriana: 'Woman of the Adriatic' or 'woman of the dark sea'. This feminine version of the Latin Adrian, refers to a native of the Roman seaport of Adria. Shakespeare used this lovely name in *A Comedy of Errors*.

Also Adria, Adrianna, Adrianne, Adrienne.

Agatha: Greek, meaning 'good woman'. St Agatha was a martyr, and it is believed her veil saved Sicily when Mount Etna erupted. This name was popularised by the prolific British author of detective fiction, Dame Agatha Mary Clarissa Christie.

Agnes: Derived from the Greek word meaning 'pure' or 'chaste', the popularity of Agnes has never waned in Scotland where the short form is Nessie.

Ailsa: See Elsa.

Aithne (eth'ni): Derived from a Celtic word, *aodnait* meaning 'little fire', this was commonly used in Ireland for baby girls with red hair.

Modern variations are Ethne and Eithne.

Aimée: See Amy.

Alana: A Celtic word meaning 'bright, fair one', often used by the Irish as a term of endearment. Alana is the feminine form of Alan.

Also Alanna, Alina, Lana, Lane.

Alberta: Feminine form of Albert, this Teutonic name means 'noble and bright', and was very popular after the marriage of Queen Victoria to Prince Albert.

Alethea: Greek word meaning 'truth'. Charles I, as Prince of Wales, courted the Spanish Princess Maria Aletea, and although she did not become his Queen, this famous courtship made her name popular in the seventeenth century. A popular name in Ireland still, with the pet form of Letty.

Alexandra: The feminine form of the Greek Alexander which means 'protector of men'. A common name earlier this century as a compliment to Queen Alexandra, wife of Edward VII, it is again popular today.

Also Alex, Alexa, Alexia, Alexis, Lexie, Sandra, Sandy and Zandra. Alexandria*

Alfreda: Another of the boy/girl names, this is one of the greatest 'elf' names passed down to us from Norse mythology, and common in England at the time of Alfred the Great. A popular shortened form is Elva.

Alice: A popular name through the ages, but one with an obscure history. In Greek the meaning is 'truth'; it is the old German word for 'nobility' and old French for 'noble and kind'.

The great revival of Alice came with Lewis Carroll's *Alice in Wonderland*, and its popularity has never waned. Other forms are Alicia, Alize, Alyce, Alysia and Lycia.

Alison: Meaning 'son of Alice' this is the Gaelic form of Alice. Particularly popular in Scotland through the ages where its other accepted forms are Alisoun and Allyson. Pet forms include Ali, Allie and Ally.

Allegra: A musical Italian name poets Byron and Longfellow each gave to his daughter, meaning 'joyful and cheerful'.

Allira: An Aboriginal name which means 'quartz'.

Aloha: The Hawaiian word for 'greetings' and 'farewell', it also means 'love and kindness'.

Alpha: Greek, for 'the first', and an obvious name for a first daughter. The Romans gave 'numeral' names to their children, as do the Balinese.

Althea: 'A healer' or 'healthy', this name was given to the Queen of Calydon in mythology. It is the botanical family name for the hollyhock. The diminutive form is Thea.

Alvira: See Elvira.

Alyssa: Greek, meaning 'sane one'. Alyssum, the small purple and white flower, derives its name from Alyssa.

Amanda: Middle Latin, meaning 'worthy of love', with the short form Mandy.

Amber: Arabic jewel name describes resin, polished to make jewellery and ornaments. This name has been popular since the publication of the novel *Forever Amber* in the 1940s.

Amelia: Meaning 'industrious one', this Teutonic name was introduced into Britain under the Hanoverian royal line and was then anglicised to Emily.

Amelia was a popular name earlier this century, which is why there are so many grandmothers and great-aunts named Amelia. It is again popular, and has the pet forms of Melo, Millie or Milly.

Other variants are Amalia, Amalie, Ameline, Amelita, Emeline, Emelia.

Amethyst: 'Of the colour of wine', this jewel is the

birthstone for girls born in February. The ancient Greeks believed this stone had the power to ward off intoxication.
Amy: From the French Aimée, meaning 'beloved'. A popular name in nineteenth-century novels (Charles Dickens's *Little Dorrit* and Lousia May Alcott's *Little Women*), it is again a favourite today.

Other forms are Amata, Amie, Amity, Amoretta, Amorita, Esmé.
Annabelle: This combination of Ann and Belle means 'graceful and beautiful'.

Also Anabel, Anabella, Annabel, Annabella, and possibly Arabella.
Anastasia: Greek, meaning 'resurrection' or 'she who will rise again', this is a popular name for an Easter baby.

The most famous and perhaps aptly named was the youngest daughter of Nicholas II, the last Czar of Russia. The Grand Duchess Anastasia was believed to have been executed after the Russian Revolution, although a Mrs Anna Anderson claimed from 1920 that she was Anastasia. This claim was officially rejected in 1961.

Other forms are Anastasie, Anstace, Anstice, Anstyce, Stacie,* Stacy. Stacey.
Andrea: Feminine of the Greek Andreas, meaning 'the man' or 'manly' – Andrea is 'the woman' or 'feminine'. Its popularity spread with the Christian faith in honour of the apostle Andrew.

Angela: 'Bringer of good tidings' or 'heavenly messenger', this is the feminine of the Greek *angelo*, for angel.

Other forms are Angelina, Angeline or Angie.

Anh: Vietnamese for a flower.

Anita: Hebrew for 'grace', this Spanish diminutive of Ann has become popular since World War II.

Ann(e): Derived from the Hebrew name 'Hannah' meaning 'full of grace'. There has long been a belief that Anne was the name of the mother of the Virgin Mary.

The name was carried back to England by the Crusaders and has been borne by six Queens of England. Queen Elizabeth II named her daughter Anne Elizabeth Alice Louise in October 1950, causing a new surge of popularity.

Ann has often formed parts of compounds such as Mary Ann (which became Marian or Marianne). Pet forms are Annie, Nan, Nancy, Nanette, Nanny. There are many variants including Anita, Anna, Annetta, Annette, Anona, Nanette.

Anthea: From the Greek meaning 'of the flowers', it has become associated with spring.

Antonia: Latin and Italian feminine forms of Antony meaning 'beyond price' or 'inestimable'. In French, Antoinette.

Other forms are Anthonia, Antoni, Netta, Netti, Netty, Toinette, Toni.

April: Latin, meaning 'the open' and signifying the beginning of spring in the northern hemisphere.

This is the first month of the Roman calendar. Like May and June, it has been used as a girl's name this century.

It sometimes has the French spelling Avril – which is a better choice if your surname is Showers!

Arabella: See Annabelle.

Areta: Meaning 'virtue' or 'value', this is still a popular Greek name.

Other forms are Arete, Aretha, Aretta, Arette.

Ariadne: Meaning 'holy' or 'divine'. In Greek mythology Ariadne helped Theseus to kill the Minotaur and escape from its labyrinth.

Also Ariane, Arianna.

Ariella: Hebrew feminine word for Ariel meaning 'lioness of God'. An appropriate name for a little lady born under the sign of Leo.

Ashleigh/Ashley: Old English, meaning 'of the ash tree'.

Astrid: Old German name meaning 'divine strength' which has always been very popular in Scandinavia.

The popularity of the name was increased by the much-loved Belgian Queen Astrid who died in a motor accident in 1935.

Atalanta: In Greek mythology Atalanta was a swift-footed huntress who promised to marry any man who could outrun her. Hippomenes took up her challenge, carrying three of the sacred apples of Hera. He dropped these one by one to distract her, won the race and Atalanta.

Athena: Meaning wisdom, from the Greek goddess.

Audrey: Originally this was an Anglo-Saxon name, Aethelthryth, which survived the Norman Conquest as Etheldreda.

The meaning is 'noble strength' which well describes the Anglo-Saxon saint Etheldreda, otherwise know as St Audrey (or Awdry).

Augusta: This is the feminine version of Augustus and is from the Latin for 'the high or august'. Pet forms are Gus or Gussie.

Aurora: In Roman mythology she was the goddess of the dawn who mourned her son's death with daily tears, hence the morning dew.

Other forms are Aurore, Ora.

Aveline: See Hazel.

Azaria: From the Hebrew masculine form, Azariah, which means 'whom God aids'.

B

Babette: See Barbara.

Barbara: Greek name meaning 'strange' or 'foreign'. Barbara, one of the great virgin saints, was beheaded by her father, who was in turn struck by lightning! Therefore Barbara protects against lightning. She is also the patron saint of architects, engineers and miners. Also Babette, Babs, Barb.

Basilia: Greek feminine form of Basil, which means 'the kingly or royal'. This plant name honours the sweet-smelling summer herb, basil.

Bathsheba: Hebrew, 'daughter of a vow' or 'seventh daughter'. Bathsheba was wife of King David and mother of King Solomon.

Beatrice: From the Latin, 'she who brings joy'. Literary connections include Dante's Beatrice Portinari in *The Divine Comedy* and Shakespeare's Beatrice in *Much Ado About Nothing*. Queen Victoria chose Beatrice for her ninth, and last, child, and the present Duke and Duchess of York for their first.

Bea, Beatty and Trixie are shorter forms.

Becky: See Rebecca.

Belinda: From the Old German, *lindi*, for serpent, the symbol of wisdom. Belinda has gained popularity in English-speaking countries over the last two hundred years.

Other forms are Belynda, Bindi, Linda, Lindy.

Belle: French for 'beautiful', in Italian, it is Bella. See Annabelle and Mirabel.

Benedicta/Benita: Feminine of the Latin Benedict, 'the blessed'.

Bernadette: From the masculine Bernard, which in Old High German means 'hard bear'.

This is a popular name for Catholic girls in honour of Marie Bernadette Soubirous (1844–79), St Bernadette of Lourdes, a French peasant girl who believed she saw visions of the Virgin Mary telling her of the healing powers of the waters at Lourdes.

Other forms are Bernadine, Bernadot, Bernetta.

Bernice: Greek for 'bringer of victory'. Bernice is

mentioned in the Bible as Herod's daughter.

Also Berenice, Berneice. Short forms are Berry, Necie, Nicie.

Bertha: In Old High German the meaning is 'the bright'. This name was a favourite in medieval Europe, then enjoyed a revival in the nineteenth century by the Victorians.

Also Berta, Bertina.

Beryl: From the Greek meaning 'precious jewel' or 'precious stone'. This blue-green stone is said to bring good luck, therefore the bearer of this name is said to have good fortune. A popular name during the Edwardian period when jewel names were fashionable.

Bessie: See Elizabeth.

Beth: See Elizabeth.

Bethany: This Hebrew name means 'worshipper of God', and is the name of a village on the west bank of the river Jordan. Also Bethanie.

Betty/Bettina: See Elizabeth and Tina.

Beulah: In Hebrew this means 'the married one', and was also the biblical term for the land of Israel.

Beverley: Anglo-Saxon, meaning 'from the beaver's lea'. Also used for boys, often as Beverly.

Bianca: Italian, meaning 'white', and in French, Blanche. In Shakespeare's *Taming of the Shrew* Bianca is the more placid sister of Kate, the shrew.

Bindi: See Belinda.

Birgitta: See Bridget.

Blanche: See Bianca.

Bliss: This is Anglo-Saxon and means 'perfect joy'. A name favoured by the English Puritans for its suggestion of heaven.

Blodwen: Welsh, meaning 'white flower'.

Bonnie: Latin name meaning 'good', and used in Scotland as a noun and an adjective. Another form is Bonita.

Brenda: Feminine of the Teutonic Brand, meaning 'a fire-brand or sword'. Brenda is the feminine form of Brendan, the patron saint of Irish sailors.

Briana: Feminine of the Celtic Brian ('strength'). Also Brenna.

Bridget: This name comes from the Celtic goddess of fire, light and poetry. St Bridget, one of the patron saints of Ireland, has helped to make this a very 'Irish' name; actress Brigitte Bardot made the French version known throughout the world, and there have been other actresses who have made the 'Brit' form popular. Others are Birgitta, Britt, Brita, Brigitta, Biddie, Brigid, Bridie.

Briony: See Bryony.

Bronwen: This Welsh name means 'the white bosomed'. On the other hand Branwen is 'dark haired'. It is amazing the difference in colour one vowel makes.

Brooke: An Old English name originally used for both sexes, meaning 'reward, enjoyment'.

Bryony: Old English, meaning 'to swell or grow bigger', this is the botanical name for a climbing plant with poisonous berries. Also Briony.

C

Caitlin: An Irish form of Catherine.

Camilla: Originally an Etruscan masculine or feminine name meaning 'attendant at religious ceremonies'. In Roman mythology this was the name of the goddess Diana's attendant.

Also popular in the French version, Camille. Diminutives are Millie, Milly.

Candace: Greek, meaning 'glittering white'. Shaw's *Candida*, published in 1898, revived the popularity of this name and its variations.

Also Candice, Candide, Candy and Daisy.

Cara: Celtic for 'friend', and Italian for 'dearest one', this name is sometimes used as a diminutive of Caroline.

Also Carina, Carita.

Carissa: From the Latin, meaning 'artful or skilful'.

Carlotta: See Charlotte.

Carly: Meaning 'free woman', this German name has gained great popularity in Australia.

Also Carla, Carley, Carlita, Karla.

Carma: Sanskrit, meaning 'destiny', from the Buddhist *karma*, or fate.

Carmel: A Hebrew name which means 'vineyard', it honours a mountain in Israel which is dedicated to the Virgin Mary. It is believed she visited there with the infant Jesus.

Also Carmela, Carmelina, Carmeline, Carmelita, Melina.

Carmen: Latin, honouring one with a beautiful voice and meaning 'songstress'. Bizet's *Carmen*, about a sensuous gipsy woman, is one of the world's best-loved operas.

Carol: 'To sing joyously', this Old French name is favoured for Christmas babies. Also a diminutive of Caroline.

Caroline: The feminine form of Carolus, the Latin version of the Old German word *carl,* meaning 'the strong or manly'.

Caroline became fashionable in the eighteenth century after Caroline of Ansbach married George II of England and became Queen.

Other forms are Carolina, Carolyn, Karolyn, Charleen, Sharleen, Sharlene. Caddie, Cara, Carol and Carrie are popular shortened forms. See also Lina.

Casey: The Irish name for boys and girls means 'courageous, brave'. It was made famous in America by Casey Jones, the train engineer who saved passengers' lives after an accident to the Cannon Ball Express.

Cassandra: 'Confuser of men' is the meaning of this Greek name. In Greek myths Cassandra was given powers of prophecy by Apollo. He changed this gift to a curse when she was unfaithful, and from then on her prophecies and warnings were disbelieved.

This has become fashionable recently, especially

in the shortened version, Cassie.

Catherine: One of the most popular girls' names over many centuries, the origin is Greek and the meaning is 'pure'.

In the fourth century Catherine was tortured on a spiked wheel, inspiring a medieval cult following. Hence the wheel-shaped firework, the Catherine wheel. Three of the six wives of Henry VIII were called Catherine, making this a well-known Tudor name.

Kathleen is the favourite variation in Ireland, and many other countries have their own forms. Catherina, Cathleen, Catalina, Caterina, Caitlin, Catriona, Cathie, Cathy, Karen, Katherine, Katerine, Kateryn, Kathryn, Katrine, Katrina, Kate, Katy, Kathy, Katie, Katinka, Kit, Kitty.

Catriona: See Catherine.

Cecilia: Derived from the Latin for 'blind'. This name was introduced to England by William the Conqueror, who named his daughter Cecilia. St Cecilia is the patron saint of music.

Also Cecile, Cecily, Cele, Celia, Ciel, Cissie, Sisley, Sissie.

See also Sheila.

Celeste: From the Latin for 'heavenly', this name has long been popular in France, along with its variation Celestine.

Celinda/Celina: See Selena.

Chantal: French name meaning 'singer'. Also Chantalle, Chantel, Chantelle, Shantelle.

Charity: From the Greek *charis*, meaning 'grace', this became one of the favourite Puritan virtue names because of the reference in the scriptures to faith, hope and charity.

Other forms are Charissa, Charita and Cherry.

Charlotte: Feminine form of Charles, used in Britain since Norman times, but popularised by Queen Charlotte Sophia, wife of George III.

Other variations are Carleen, Carlotta, Charlotta, Charleen, Charlene, Charlie and Lottie.

Charmaine: From the Latin meaning 'a little song', this was popular during the 1920s when Charmaine was the name of a 'hit' song, and a popular ballroom dance.

Charmian: Not to be confused with Charmaine, this name is of Greek origin and means 'joy'. Charmian is the attendant of Cleopatra in Shakespeare's play.

Chen: Chinese for precious and rare.

Cherie: French, meaning 'dear, beloved one'. Used generally as a term of endearment. Also Cheri.

Cheryl: A (1920s) French name meaning 'dear, beloved', adapted from *chère*, or 'sweet cherry' from *cerise*. It has been further anglicised to Sheryl, and both these forms were popular names of the post World War II baby boom.

Chloe: Greek, meaning 'a green shoot'. Chloe was the goddess of unripened wheat. This is one of the old names currently enjoying new popularity.

Chloris: Greek, meaning 'pale flower'. Chloris in Greek mythology was goddess of flowers who

turned pale when hunted by the sun god Apollo.
Christabel: This Greek-French combined name means 'beautiful, bright-faced Christian'.
Christine: One of the many names derived from 'Christ', the origin is Greek and means simply 'a Christian'.

Also Christina, Christiana, Chris, Chrissie, Christie, Teenie and Tina.
Chu: The Chinese word for pearl.
Cilla: Probably a diminutive of Priscilla, this name was popularised by Cilla Black, the singer of the sixties and fellow-Liverpudlian of the Beatles.
Cindy: See Lucy.
Cissie: See Cecilia.
Clarabelle: A Latin-French combination name of Clare, 'the clear' and Belle, 'the beautiful'. Also Clarabella.
Clare: From the Latin, meaning 'bright' or 'illustrious'; this was first used in England about seven hundred years ago and has always been popular, often with the French spelling Claire. Also Clara.
Clarice: French form of Clara, 'little shining one'. Also Chlaris, Claresta, Clariss, Clarissa, Clarisse.
Clarinda: A Spanish name meaning 'shining blossom of spring', this was popular with seventeenth- and eighteenth-century poets.
Claudia: This feminine form of the Latin Claudius or Claud means 'the lame'. Also Claudette, Claudine.
Clematis: A Greek 'flower' name meaning 'the clinging', as in vine. Clem or Clemmie are shorter forms.

Clementine: 'The clement or merciful', this is the feminine form of Clement. Another of the Puritan 'virtue' names, its popularity was rekindled by the gold-miners' song, 'My Darling Clementine'.

Also Clemency, Clementia, Clementina, Clem and Clemmie, and Tina.

Cleo: This well-known abbreviation of Cleopatra is from the Greek meaning 'glory' or 'fame'. Seven of Egypt's queens bore this name, the most famous of whom was Cleopatra VII, mistress to Julius Caesar and later to Mark Antony.

Cleopatra: See Cleo.

Clodagh: An Irish name (after the river in Tipperary), this was first used by the Marquis of Waterford for his daughter. Popularity of this name has grown, but it is rarely heard outside Ireland.

Clorinda: Not to be confused with the Spanish Clarinda, the origin of this name is Persian and the meaning is 'renowned'. Use of Clorinda by Tasso, the sixteenth-century Italian poet, made it a popular name.

Clothilda/Clotilda: A Teutonic name meaning 'famous battle maiden', the first Klothilda was famous for changing the religion of Europe when, as wife of the King of the Franks, she converted him to Christianity.

Also Clothilde.

Colette: This French name honouring St Colette means 'a collar or necklace'. It is also a short form of Nicolette.

Colleen: Meaning simply 'girl', this name is still popular, especially in Ireland. Also Coleen, Colene.

Constance: Well known today in the popular shortened form, Connie, this Latin feminine form of Constantine means 'the firm or constant'. A favourite name of early Christians, then the Victorians. Also Constanzia.

Cora: From the Greek *kore*, meaning 'maiden' or 'young girl'. A popular name in Greece and in France as Corinne. Also Corinna.

Coral: A Latin 'charm' name in honour of the red Mediterranean coral worn as an amulet as protection from harm. Coral jewellery was fashionable in Victorian England, leading to the adoption of the name there.

Cordella: A medieval Welsh name for 'sea jewel'. Cordelia, in Welsh legend, was daughter of Lear, King of the Sea. The diminutive is Delia.

Corinne: See Cora.

Cosette: A Teutonic name meaning 'pet lamb', and a French term of affection! In Victor Hugo's *Les Miserables* Cosette is the foster-child of Jean Valjean.

Courtney: In Old French this grand-sounding name has the rather lowly meaning 'short nose'. Originally used only as a surname, Courtney has recently become a popular girl's name.

Crystal: Greek name meaning 'the ice-clear', the transparent quartz was popular as jewellery and became one of the Edwardian jewel names. Also Chrystal.

Cynthia: Greek, meaning 'the moon', Cynthia was another name for Artemis, the moon-goddess, in honour of her birth place, Mt Cynthus.

D

Dacia: An ancient country north of the Danube.
Dagmar: A Danish name meaning 'glory of the Danes'. Queen Dagmar made it popular in Denmark.
Dahlia: This Latin flower name means 'of the valley', and is in honour of the Swedish botanist Dahl.
Daisy: Anglo-Saxon name meaning 'day's eye', this flower name has also been used as a pet form of Margaret because the French word for daisy is *marguerite*. Also the diminutive for Candace.
Dale: An Anglo-Saxon name meaning 'valley', used for both girls and boys.
Dalila: This African name, not to be confused with the Hebrew Delilah, means 'gentle'.
Dallas: The Teutonic meaning is 'the playful', and the Old Irish is 'the skilled'. A name given to sons and daughters in the United States, where it is a place name for the Texan city and a most successful 'soap'!
Damaris: Greek, meaning 'tame' or 'gentle', this New Testament name was adopted by the Puritans in the seventeenth century. Also Damara.

21

Dana/Dane: See Danica.

Danella: See Danielle.

Danica: Norse name meaning 'the morning star'. This is becoming a popular name of the eighties, also in the shortened forms Dana and Dane.

✗Danielle: The feminine of Daniel, in Hebrew meaning 'God is my judge', and popular since the early 1970s. Also Danella, Daniela, Danita.

Daphne: Greek for 'laurel', and a flower name honouring laurel, or daphne. In Greek mythology Daphne was a mountain nymph who rejected Apollo. To escape him she was turned into a laurel tree by Gaea.

Daphna is a variation, and Daffy a pet name.

Dara: This Hebrew name means 'charity, compassion and wisdom'.

Darlene: An Anglo-Saxon name meaning 'little darling'.

Davida: See Davina.

Davina: This is the Scottish feminine of the Hebrew David, 'beloved'. Other forms are Davida, Davita, Vida, Vita.

Dawn: Anglo-Saxon, meaning 'break of day', this name replaced Aurora, its Latin equivalent. A popular baby-boom name of the late 1940s when parents were hopeful of a new day.

Deanna: See Diana.

Deborah: 'The bee' in Hebrew, this name implies wisdom and eloquence. The name was popular with the English Puritans, and has been revived this century.

Other forms are Debbie, Debby, Debra.

Decima: From the Latin Decimus, 'the tenth', this name was given to the tenth child, if a girl, in the days when families were larger and home help was free!

Deirdre: This Old Irish name means 'sorrow' or 'broken-hearted'. The beautiful Deirdre of Irish mythology fled to Scotland with her lover. On their return to Ireland, he was put to death by the King, and Deirdre took her own life.

Delia: Greek name for the moon goddess, Artemis, who was born on the island of Delos. Also a diminutive of Cordelia.

Delilah: 'The gentle temptress', this ancient Hebrew name was that of the biblical betrayer of Samson.

Also Delila, Lila.

Delores: See Dolores.

Denise: Feminine of Dennis or Dion, from the Latin Dionysus (or Bacchus), the god of wine. Also Denice, Denys.

Desirée: A French name meaning 'desired one'.

Deva: A Sanskrit name meaning 'the divine'.

Devona: Old English, meaning 'of Devon', and popular for girls from that county.

Diana: Diana was the Roman goddess of the woodlands, the moon, hunting, wild animals, and also of chastity!

Lady Diana Frances Spencer married the Prince of Wales in 1981, causing a new wave of popularity for this name among royalists. Also Deanna, Diane, Dianna. Di is the popular short version.
Dido: See Elissa.
Dilys: A modern Welsh name meaning 'genuine' or 'perfect'. Also Delys.
Dinah: Hebrew, meaning 'the judged', this was the name of the beautiful daughter of Jacob and Leah.
Dione: A name of Greek origin, meaning 'the daughter of heaven and earth'.
Dolly: See Dorothy.
Dolores: Of Latin origin, meaning 'grief' or 'pain', this popular Spanish name commemorates the seven sorrows in the life of the Virgin Mary. Also Delores.
Dominique: Feminine of Dominic, meaning 'belonging to the Lord', this has been a popular name since the founding of the order of the Dominicans in the thirteenth century.
Donna: Italian for 'refined lady', and implies a woman worthy of respect.
Dora: See Dorothy.
Dorcas: From the Greek, meaning gazelle.
Doreen: Of French origin, this name means 'the gold or gilded'. C. J. Dennis's highly successful *The Songs of a Sentimental Bloke* included the serenade to the Bloke's beloved Doreen, making this a popular name after the book's publication in 1915.
Dorinda: 'The beautiful' in Greek, this is a popular Spanish name.

Doris: Meaning 'of the ocean'. In Greek mythology Doris was a sea nymph and daughter of Oceanus, god of the sea. She was the wife of Nereus, to whom she bore fifty golden-haired sea nymphs. Dodi is a pet form.

Dorothy: From the Greek for 'God's gift', this name has been in use since the fifteenth century. Its popularity peaked in the 1930s after Judy Garland's Dorothy in *The Wizard of Oz*.

Other forms are Doll, Dolly, Dora, Doretta, Dorothea, Dot, Dotty, Thea, Theodora.

Drusilla: 'The strong one' in Latin.

Dulcie: A Latin name meaning 'sweet and charming', this is also the diminutive form of Dulcinea, the love of Don Quixote. Also Dulcia, Dulciana.

E

Eartha: An old English name meaning 'of the earth', it is appropriate for the talented singer with the earthy voice, Eartha Kitt.

Eden: Hebrew for 'pleasure' or 'a place of pleasure', this name honours the garden where, according to the Bible, the first woman and man were created.

Edith: An Anglo-Saxon name meaning 'the rich, prosperous and happy'. This name survived the Norman Conquest and was one of the most popular of English names during the nineteenth century.

Also Eadith, Eadie, Eda, Ede.
Edmonda: Feminine form of the Anglo-Saxon Edmond, meaning 'prosperous protector'.
Edna: This is Hebrew for 'rejuvenation', a state all parents at some stage wish to experience.
Edwina: Feminine of the Anglo-Saxon Edwin, meaning 'prosperous friend'. This name is always popular in Scotland, and now in Australia.
Effie: A popular Greek name from Euphemia, meaning 'pleasant speech'.
Eileen: Developed from the Irish *eibhlin* and *ailbhlin*, this name means 'life-giving' or 'light-giving'. Aileen is the Scottish form.

Other variations are Eilleen, Elain, Elaine, Ilene.
Elaine: See Eileen, and Helen.
Eleanor: This was the Provençal variant of Helen, used in England since Henry II's marriage to Eleanor of Aquitaine in 1152. Diminutives are Ella and Nora.
Electra: A Greek name meaning 'the brilliant one'.
Elissa: Of Phoenician origin, this is another name for Dido, Queen of Carthage. In Greek legend she fled to the African coast after her brother, Pygmalion, murdered her husband. There she founded the city of Carthage.
Eliza: A form of Elizabeth, now considered an independent name. After Mary, this was the most common name in Victorian England.
Elizabeth: Hebrew for 'God has sworn' or 'oath of God', this name has enjoyed popularity for centuries

and is, of course, a royal favourite. Of all names it seems this one has the longest list of variants and pet forms.

The alternative spelling is Elisabeth and the many variants include Bess, Bessie, Bet, Beth, Bettina, Bettisa, Betsy, Betty; Elise, Elisa, Elissa, Eliza, Elyssa; Libby, Lilibet, Lis, Lisa, Lisabet, Lisabetta, Lisabette, Lisbeth, Lisette, Lissie, Liz, Liza, Lizette, Lizzie . . .

Ella: Anglo-Saxon name meaning 'beautiful fairy maiden'. Also a diminutive form of Eleanor and Helen.

Ellen: Early English form of Helen.

Elmira: Feminine of the Anglo-Saxon Elmer, meaning 'of noble fame'. Almira in Arabic means 'princess'; in both languages this is feminine for prince or emir.

Eloise: See Louise.

Elsa: From the Old German for 'noble maiden'. The Scottish form Ailsa is also popular.

Elva: See Alfreda.

Elvira: Originally from *alba*, Latin for 'white', variations spread widely. This version is most popular in Spain. Also Albina, Alvira, Elvire.

Elysia: In Greek mythology, the Elysian fields were places of pleasure and happiness for the gods.

Emily: Meaning 'industrious', this English form of Amelia came into English usage in the eighteenth century. George II's daughter Emilia was known as Emily, making this an independent name.

See also Ilka.

Emma: A Teutonic name for 'all-embracing' or 'universal one'. This was a popular name after publication last century of Jane Austen's novel *Emma*. Again a fashionable name, other forms are Emmeline, Emeline, Emelina.

Ena: This Gaelic name, meaning 'ardent' or 'fiery one', was popular earlier this century because of Princess Victoria Ena, granddaughter of Queen Victoria, and later Queen of Spain.

Enid: Celtic name meaning 'purity of the soul'.

Eranthe: A Greek flower name for the aromatic spring-flowering herb, chamomile.

Erica: Modern girl's name which is feminine of the Old Norse Eric, 'the regal'. In botany *erica* is the heath.

Also Erika, Ricky.

Esmé: Meaning 'beloved', this originated as a French variation of Amy.

Estelle: See Esther.

Esther: Persian name for 'a star', the equivalent to the Latin Stella. This can be traced to the Babylonian goddess of love, Ishtar.

There are many forms including the French Estelle, Italian Ester, and Spanish Estella or Estrellita. Hestia, Hester and Hetty are English short forms. See also Hadassah.

Ethel: Anglo-Saxon name meaning 'noble maiden', which was originally a diminutive of other nobility names like Ethelfleda, Ethelburga, Etheldreda, Etheldrid and Ethelinda.

Ethne/Eithne: See Aithne.
Eugenia: Feminine of the Greek Eugene, meaning 'the well born'. The French form became popular in France after the Empress Eugenie, wife of Napoleon III.
Eunice: Greek for 'happy victory'.
Euphemia: See Effie.
Eve: Hebrew, meaning 'life'; the biblical Eve was the first woman, wife and mother. The name Eve was believed to bring longevity.
 Also Eva, Evalina, Evelyn, Evita. See also Lina.
Evelyn: See Eve, and Hazel.
Evonne: Ten-year-old Evonne Goollagong left her NSW country home town of Barellan to live and train with her coach, Vic Edwards, in Sydney. She went on to win thirty-seven Australian junior titles. Aged nineteen, she won her first Wimbledon in 1971, and in 1980 became the first mother to win the title. See Yvonne.

F

Fabia: The Fabian family were wealthy bean growers of Ancient Rome. Also Fabian, Fabiola, Fabienne.
Fabian: See Fabia.
Faith: Latin for 'to trust', this name honours the first of the three Christian virtues, Faith, Hope and

Charity. One of the names made popular by the Puritans. Also Fae, Fay, Faye.
Fay/Faye: See Faith.
Fayme: An Old English name from the Latin *fama*, meaning 'fame'. The French version is Fameuse.
Felicity: Feminine of the Latin *felix*, meaning 'happy'. The Roman goddess of good luck, Felicitas, became known in Britain as Felice. Felicia was the popular version last century, and Felicity in the twentieth.

Also Felicita, Felicitia, and the short form, Fee.
Fenella: In Gaelic this means 'white-shouldered'. Finella is the Irish version, and the Old Celtic is Fynvola.
Fern: Anglo-Saxon, from the Sanskrit, 'a wing or feather'.
Fidella: Feminine of the Latin Fidel, meaning 'faithful'. Another of the Puritan virtue names.
Fina: See Seraphina.
Fiona: From the Gaelic, meaning 'fair one' or 'white one', this name was originally Fionn. Fiona was first used at the turn of the century, and has been very popular in Australia in the last twenty years.
Fiorella: See Florence.
Flavia: Meaning 'blond or yellow-haired', this is a common Roman name; in French Flavie.
Fleur: The French word for flower.
Flora: See Florence.
Florence: Latin for 'to flower or flourish'. The Italian city of Florence, noted for its flowers, was

named after Flora, the Roman goddess of flowers and all blooming vegetation. Also Flora, Florice, Florene, Florette, Florinda, Fiorella.
Frances: Meaning 'from France', this has been the name of many saints and kings in the masculine form, Francis. The Spanish Francisca and French Francesca have long been popular names. The shortened forms are Frankie and Francie.
Freda: German name meaning 'peace', for one who is calm. Also a diminutive of Frederica.
Frederica: Feminine of the German Frederick, meaning 'rich peace'.
Freya: In Old Norse mythology Freyja was the goddess of love and fertility.

G

Gabrielle: 'Woman of God', this is the feminine form of the Hebrew Gabriel, honouring the archangel of the Annunciation. Other forms are Gabriella, Gabriela, Gabrilla. Gaby or Gabby are popular short versions.
Gaea: In Greek mythology Gaia was the goddess of the earth. Gaea and Gaia are both used in English.
Gai: French name meaning 'lively'. The English spelling is Gay.
Gail/Gale: An Anglo-Saxon name meaning 'to sing', used through the centuries for girls and boys. The

feminine versions, Gail and Gayle, are also the diminutives of Abigail.

Garda/Gerda: This Old High German name, which means 'the protected', is from the same word as 'garden'. Very popular in Norway, it is also used widely in France as Garde and Gerde.

Gemma: A name which has been popular for centuries. In Latin the meaning is 'precious stone' or 'trinket'. Other forms are Gemmie or Gemsie.

Genevieve: One of the group of Celtic 'white' names from Gwen; Genevieve, patron saint of Paris, is the French version.

Also Guinevere, Gwendolen, Gwynne, and Jennifer.

Georgia/Georgina: Feminine form of Greek George, meaning 'a husbandman or worker of the earth'. The English used Georgiana in honour of the Georgian kings.

Also Georgana, Georgene, Georgette, Georgie, Georgy, Gina and Girogia.

Geraldine: Feminine form of Gerald, in Old High German 'the spear wielder'. Other forms are Geralda, Geraldina, Gerhardine, Jeraldine. Pet names are Gerry or Jerry.

Germaine: The literal meaning is 'of Germany'.

Gertrude: Old High German for 'the spear maiden'. Gertrude, in Norse mythology, was one of the Valkyries who carried the souls of the dead to Valhalla. This is not one of the popular names of this era; however the shortened versions, Truda, Trudi or Trudy are often used.

Gilberta: This is the feminine form of Gilbert, and is Old High German meaning 'bright of will'. This is one of the few male/female names where the feminine is the older.

Also Gilberte, Gilbertina, Gilbertine.

Gilda: An Anglo-Saxon word meaning 'the gilded or golden'.

Gillian: A common medieval name from the Latin for 'young nestling', with the pet form of Gill, often spelt Jill. The word Jill became synonymous with sweetheart, hence the expression 'every Jack has his Jill'. Other forms are Gill, Gillie, Jill, Jillian, Jillie.

Giselle: Teutonic word meaning 'pledge' or 'a hostage', a name which conjures up pictures of dainty ballerinas.

Gladys: From the Latin *gladius*, 'a sword'. The Welsh is Gwladys, and other variations are Gladine, Gladusa, Gladuse.

Glenna: A very old Celtic name, this is from the masculine Glen, 'of the glen or valley'. Also Glendene, Glenda, Glendora, Glenn, Glennis.

Gloria: Latin for 'glory' or 'glorious one', a name which enjoyed great popularity earlier this century.

Godiva: Teutonic, meaning 'God's gift or love'. In the eleventh century Lady Godiva became famous when, according to legend, she rode through the streets of Coventry wearing nothing but her long hair to protest against her husband Leofric's harsh taxation.

Goldie: A real name, not a nickname as some might think, this Anglo-Saxon word means 'pure gold'. A propitious name for a baby girl.

Grace: In Latin, 'the loved, favoured, honoured'. Also Gracie, Gracienne, Gracye, Gratiana.

Griselda: Old High German name meaning 'gray battle-maid'. A popular name in Scotland where the shortened form is Grize!

Also Chriselda, Grissell, Grizzel, and Zelda.

Gudrid: An Old Norse name popular for Scandinavian girls, meaning 'divine passion'. Also Guri.

Gudrun: Old Norse name meaning 'divine wisdom'. In Teutonic mythology many tragedies of medieval Germany and Norway featured Gudrun as the heroine. Also Gudron, Gudruna, Guthrun.

Gunhild: 'Brave battle or warrior maid' this warrior-type description is typical of many of the feminine Teutonic names. Also Gunhilda, Gunhilde.

Guida: A popular Italian name meaning 'to guide'. Also Guietta, Guillena.

Guinevere: One of the Celtic 'white' names, this one meaning 'white phantom'. See also Genevieve, Gwendolen, Gwynne, and Jennifer.

Gwen/Gwendolen: In Welsh 'the white one', from which has sprung many variations; in English Genevra, Guinevere, Jennifer, and the Scottish Ginevra.

Gwynne: Popular Celtic name meaning 'white/fair'. Also Gwyn, Gwyneth, Winnie, Winny. See Genevieve, Guinevere, Jennifer.

H

Hadassah: One of the oldest Hebrew flower names, meaning 'myrtle'. In the Bible this is used as another name for Esther.

Haidee: This Greek name means 'the modest' and has been used widely by the English and French. Haidee was the Greek girl in Lord Byron's *Don Juan*.

Also Haida and Haydee.

Halona: An American-Indian name which means 'happy fortune'. Also spelt Halonna.

Hannah: See Ann(e).

Harriet: See Henrietta.

Hayley: Of Anglo-Saxon origin and meaning 'hay maiden', this name became popular in the sixties with the success of Hayley Mills, the film star.

Hazel: Anglo-Saxon for 'the hazel tree'. The ancients of north-western Europe believed that a wand of the hazel tree symbolised wisdom and protection. A fitting name for the wife of a Prime Minister!

Also Aveline (French for the hazel); this in turn became Evelyn.

Heather: Scottish flower name popular this century, it means 'flower of the moors'.

Hebe: An important Greek name meaning 'youth'. Hebe, in Greek mythology, was cup-bearer to the gods and had the power of restoring youth.

Hedda: Meaning 'war' or 'strife', this Teutonic name is a fitting one for the head-strong heroine of the Henrik Ibsen play *Hedda Gabler*, written last century. Still a popular Scandinavian name, the English adaptations are Avice, Avicia, Avise, Havoise, Heda and Hedwig. Heide is another version.

Helen: Feminine of the Greek Helenas, meaning 'light'. A much-used name in music, art and prose, and in Greek and Roman mythology. Traditionally the most beautiful woman of all was Helen of Troy, whose 'face launched a thousand ships' and whose beauty caused the Trojan war.

Some of the many variations are Helena, Eleanor, Helenora, Hellene, Lorene, Ella, Ellyn, Elyn, Ilene, Ellette, Nellette, Jelena, Jellica, Jeleta, Leonora, Lenore, Narelle, Nell, Nellie, Norah, Nora.

Helene is popular still in Greece and France, Eleonora in Italy, Eleonore in Germany, Ellenis in Spain, Ellen in Scotland, Helena and Eileen in Ireland, and Ellin in Wales.

Heloise: See Louise.

Helga: Feminine form of the Old Norse name Helgi, 'the holy'.

Heloise: See Louise.

Henrietta: Feminine of Henry in Old High German, meaning 'ruler of private property'. Harriet is the most common form of Henrietta, and the feminine of Harry. Among the many variations are Etta, Ettie, Harriote, Hattie, Hennie, Henriette, Henriqueta, Hetty, Nettie.

Hepzibah: A Hebrew name with the meaning, 'my delight is in her'. In the Bible she was Hezekiah's wife. Variations are Happy, Hep, Hepsy and Hepzibeth.

Hermione: Perhaps because the pronunciation causes some difficulty (her-my-o-nee), this Greek name is rare today. The meaning is 'noble' and it is the feminine of Hermes, one of the Greek gods.

Hester/Hettie: See Esther.

Hilary: A Greek name used for girls or boys, meaning 'the cheerful and merry'. This name honoured St Hilarius, a strong supporter of Christianity in France during the fourth century.

Hilda: In Old Anglo-Saxon, German and Norse this meant 'battle', and is typical of the Teutonic names for females. The Old Norse is Hiltrut, and other English forms are Hylda, Hildie, Hildy, Ilda, Ilde.

Hildegarde: Teutonic name meaning 'battle maiden'. St Hildegart was a twelfth-century German mystic.

Holly: Anglo-Saxon meaning 'holy', this is a plant name for the holly tree which is always associated with Christmas. As its red berries symbolise new life, this is a name well-suited to a girl born during the Christmas season.

Honey: Not just a term of endearment, but a real name with an Anglo-Saxon origin, meaning 'sweet one'.

Hope: Meaning 'to hope or cherish', this Anglo-Saxon name was popular with the Puritans.

Hortense: Feminine of the Latin name Hortensius, which means 'a gardener'.

Hyacinth: The name for the flower which in Greek mythology, sprang from the spilled blood of the young Hyacinth. Also Jacinta.

I

Ida: In Old High German this is 'the happy', in Anglo-Saxon 'the rich', and in Greek it refers to the mythological Mt Ida.

Ilka: The Scottish meaning, 'each and every one', is quite different from the Slavic 'flattering'. This is a contracted form of Emily, through the Slavic Milka.

Ilona: In Hungarian 'the beautiful', and in Greek 'the light'. Often Anglicised to Lorna.

Imogene: In Latin 'an image' or 'image of her mother', the name first appeared in Germany during the fifteenth century as Imagina.

Also Emogene, Imelda, Imogine.

Ina: Although often used as a complete name, this is actually a Latin suffix found in many Spanish and Italian names such as Rosina and Wilhelmina. In the Filipino dialect, Tagalog, Ina is 'mother'.

Indira: A Sanskrit name meaning 'an Indian goddess'.

Indra: Hindustani, meaning 'the thunder'. Indra was the thunder god in Hindu religion. Also Indred.

Ingrid: Old Norse, 'Ing's daughter'. In Norse mythology Ing was a god of fertility, prosperity and peace, and was a great hero.

Also Inga, Ingar, Ingeborg, Ingunna.

Iola/Iole: From the Greek, meaning 'dawn cloud'. In Greek mythology Hercules fell in love with Princess Iole and captured her.

Iolanthe: Greek name meaning 'violet flower'. The popularity of this name in England was due to Gilbert & Sullivan's light opera *Iolanthe*. Also Iolanda, Yolanda, Yolande.

Irene: Greek origin, meaning 'peace'. Eirene, in Greek mythology, and Eir, in Norse mythology, were goddesses of peace. The Old Norse version is still in use today.

Other variations are Eirena, Erena, Irena, Irina, Rene. The Russian name is Eereenia, and is in common usage.

Iris: From the Greek word for 'rainbow'. In Greek mythology Iris was the fleet-footed messenger of the gods.

Irma: Teutonic meaning is 'strong', and in Latin 'noble person'.

Isa: This Teutonic name means 'the iron-like', also diminutive for Isabel.

Isabel: Spanish form of Elizabeth.

Isadora: From the Greek meaning 'the gift of Isis'. Isis, the goddess of fruitfulness, flooded the Nile with her tears, making the land of Egypt fertile.

The American dancer, Isadora Duncan, who was

greatly admired for her innovative modern dance methods and bohemian lifestyle, increased the popularity of this name. She died in 1927 at the age of 49 when her long scarf became entangled in the wheel of her car.

Ita: A Gaelic name meaning 'desire for truth'. Ita Clare Buttrose was born on 17 January 1942, and is well known as a journalist, editor, publisher, radio broadcaster and television compere.

Ivy: This is another plant name of the Greeks who considered the vine sacred to Bacchus. A wreath of ivy hanging outside a Greek inn was a sign that wine was sold within. Also Ivana, Ive, Ivis.

J

Jacinta/Jacinth: See Hyacinth.

Jacqueline/Jacobina/Jamesina: Feminine form of the Hebrew for Jacob, meaning 'the supplanter'. Jacqueline is the French feminine form of Jacques. Jacob and James are common forms of one another, hence Jacobina and Jamesina.

Among the many variations and diminutive forms are Jacalyn, Jackie, Jacquenella, Jacquetta and Jimmie. The French also use Jacquenette, Jacquette and Jacobee; the German form is Jakobine; the Dutch is Jacomina, and the Russian Jacovina or Zakelina.

Jade: From the Latin *jada*, meaning 'the jade'. The Chinese meaning is 'love'; the Chinese believe jade to be the emblem of long life and good luck. The Spanish called the glowing green mineral 'pain in the side', believing it had the ability to cure pain.

Jan/Janice/Janis: See Jane.

Jane: Along with Jean, Joanna and Joan, this is the feminine form of the Hebrew name John, meaning 'God is gracious'. Defying fads and fashions, this has been one of the most consistently popular of all girls' names.

In the twelfth century Europe began using Joanna, which in Spanish became Juana, and in French Jehanne. The very old English form is Jhone and other English forms are Johanna, Joanna, Joanne, Jonita, Joanie, Janna, Janelle, Jayne, Janet, Janette, Jean, Jeanette, Jeanine, Janine, Janina, Janice, Janis, Jan. The Italian forms, Giovanna and Gianina, and the Spanish, Juanita, are in common usage. Ivanka is the Yugoslav form.

The Irish version Siobhán (pronounced 'Shoo-vawn' with the stress on the second syllable), has long been a favourite girls' name in Ireland.

See also Shane and Sheena.

Janelle/Janella: See Jane.

Janina: In Sanskrit this means 'the kind'. Also an English variant of Jane.

Janine: See Jane.

Janna/Jannah: A Hebrew name meaning 'the Lord gave'. Also a form of Jane.

Jarita: A Hindustani name meaning 'the bird'. In

Hindu mythology, the bird Jarita was so protective of her babies she was given a woman's soul and became human.

Jarvia: Another of the Teutonic battle-maiden names, this is the feminine form of Jarvis, which means 'sharp as a spear'.

Jasmine: A Persian flower name. Also Jessamine.

Jayne: In Sanskrit the meaning is 'God's victorious smile'. Also a variation of Jane.

Jean/Jeanette/Jeanine: See Jane, Netta and Sheena.

Jemima: In Hebrew this is 'the dove', the symbol of peace. The biblical Jemima was the daughter of Job.

Longfellow's poem referring to 'a little girl, who had a little curl, right in the middle of her forehead', was about a Jemima!

Other variations are Jemimah, Jem, Jemmie and Mima.

Jennifer/Jenny: See Genevieve.

Jeremia: The feminine of the Hebrew Jeremiah, 'the Lord's exalted'. Shortened versions are Jeri, Jerrie, Jerry. The Italian form is Geremia.

Jessmine: See Jasmine.

Jessica: Feminine form of the Hebrew Jesse, meaning 'God's grace' or 'the rich'. The biblical Jesse was David's father. Shakespeare was probably responsible for introducing the name to England through the daughter of Shylock in *The Merchant of Venice*. Also Jess, Jessie, Jesslyn.

Jezebel: Hebrew, meaning 'devotee of Baal', a false god. Jezebel in the Bible 'painted her face ... and looked out of the window'. Hence a bold woman is known as 'a Jezebel'.

Jill/Jillian: See Gillian.

Joan/Joanna: See Jane.

Jocelyn: Probably from the Latin Justus, through the Welsh, this is both a male and female name, as is Joyce. Variants are Jocelin, Joceline, Jodoca, Joscelind, Joscelyn, Justine.

Jodi/Jodie: See Judith.

Josephine: This is the French feminine of the Hebrew name Joseph, 'he shall add'. In honour of the husband of Mary, Germany used Josepha and France Josephe.

Napoleon's Empress was actually baptized Josephe, the Josephine is a diminutive form.

Other variants are Jo, Josephina, Josette, Josephie, Josie. The French also use Fifi and Fifine, the Italians Giuseppina, and the Spanish Josefa and Pepita.

Joy: In Latin this means 'joy' or 'to rejoice'. One of the old English virtue names favoured by the Puritans. Also Joyce.

Joyce: See Jocelyn and Joy.

Juanita: See Jane.

Judith: Hebrew, meaning 'woman of Judaea'.

The name became known in England in the ninth century. Judith, mother of Alfred the Great, set her sons a reading competition, which is said to have started Alfred's interest in education.

The diminutive Judy has been popular in England

since around 1700, when the first Punch and Judy show was performed.

Other shortened forms are Judi, Judie, Jodie. The German versions are Juditha, Jutha and Jutta, French is Judithe, and the Italian Giuditta.

Julia: Feminine of the Latin Julius or Julian and a popular name for girls born in July. The diminutive form, Juliet, was made famous by Shakespeare.

Other variants are Juliana, Julietta, Julita, Julie, Julyan.

June: In fairly recent use as a girl's name it is associated with the month of June.

Juno: In Roman mythology Juno was Jupiter's wife and the queen of heaven.

Justine: See Jocelyn.

K

Kama: A Sanskrit name meaning 'love'. Kama is the Hindu god of love who, like the Greek Cupid, carried a bow.

Kamania: An African name meaning 'like the moon'.

Karen: One of the many variations of Catherine, this is Danish. Also Kara, Karena.

Karma: From the Sanskrit, meaning 'destiny'. Also Carma.

Katherine/Katinka/Kate: See Catherine and Kay.

Kathleen: See Catherine.

Katrina: See Catherine.

Kay: Often used as a diminutive of Katherine, but also as a separate name.

Keely: 'The beautiful one', a Gaelic name for beautiful girls. Also Keele.

Keiko: A Japanese name meaning 'beloved'.

Kelly: A Gaelic name meaning 'warrior maid', which despite its meaning is very popular.

Kelsey: Meaning 'from the island'; this is an Old Norse name.

Kendra/Kenna: An Anglo-Saxon name meaning 'knowing or understanding'.

Kerry: Of Celtic origin, meaning 'the dark'. There is an Irish county called Kerry. The kerry was also an apron.

Ketura: A Hebrew word meaning 'incense'. This is one of the Biblical names used by the English Puritans. Also Keturah.

Keziah: In Hebrew 'the cassia tree'. The biblical Keziah was one of Job's daughters. Also Kazia, Ketsy, Kezia, Kissy, Kitsy.

Kieren: A Celtic name meaning 'black', and acceptable for girls and boys. Also Kieron.

Kiki: Egyptian name meaning 'the castor plant'. This plant is highly ornamental as well as having a medicinal value.

Kim: Although the origin is unknown, the meaning of this short and sweet name is 'ruler'. A name for boys and girls. Also a pet form of Kimberley.

Kimberley: An English name meaning 'from the

royal meadow', this first became popular for girls in Victorian times. See Kim.

Kineta: A Greek word meaning 'active'.

Kiri: A Maori name meaning 'tree bark', to which New Zealand's famous opera singer Dame Kiri Te Kanawa has brought great popularity. Also Kirilees, Kirilly, Kirri.

Kirsten: The Norse meaning is 'the annointed one', and literally 'a Christian'. This is the Scandinavian version of Christine. Also Kirstie, Kirstin, Kirsty, Kristin, Kristie.

Kitty: See Catherine.

Krishna: This Sanskrit name honours the most celebrated of Hindu deities. The meaning literally is 'dark or black'.

Kylie: This Aboriginal name, meaning 'boomerang', is the first name of two famous and popular Australian women, Minogue and Mole.

Kyna: Taken from the Welsh masculine form of Kynan or Conan, which means 'the wise' or 'chief'. The feminine meaning is 'wise lady'.

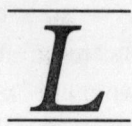

L

Laelia/Lelia: The name Lelia became popular through a novel by the French writer George Sand. Other English forms are Lela, Lelah and in French Lelia and Lelie.

Lais: Meaning 'rejoice', this is a popular Greek name, as legend tells of Lais of Corinth who was considered the most beautiful of all beautiful women!

Lakshmi: A Sanskrit name honouring the Hindu goddess of success and beauty.

Lala: A Slavic name for 'tulip'.

Lana: See Alana.

Lani: A Maori name meaning 'flower', originating from the Hawaiian islands.

Lara: A Latin name meaning 'famous'. Lara was a talkative nymph who prattled so much she was punished by Jove! Also Larentia, Laretta.

Laura: From the same root as Laurence, a wreath of woven laurel was a prize of victory awarded to heroes and poets.

The many English variations include Laurinda, Lauretta, Laurel, Laureen, Lauren, Lora, Loren, Lorinda, Lorna, Lori, Lorrie, Loris and Loretta. The Latin is Laurentia, Italian Lorenza, and French Laure and Laurette.

Laurel: See Laura.

Lauren: See Laura.

Layla: An African name meaning 'born at night'.

Lea: This Anglo-Saxon name which means 'the lea or grassland', is a popular girl/boy name of today. Also Lee, Leigh.

Leah: Hebrew name meaning 'the weary one'. In the Bible Leah was Jacob's wife. Lia, in Italian, was one of Dante's heroines.

Leala: Old French name meaning 'faithful'.

Leanne: A combination of two girls' names – Lee and Anne. See Liana.

Lee: See Lea.

Leigh: See Lea.

Leilani: The Hawaiian name, meaning 'heavenly blossom', describes the tropical flower of the Islands. Also Lullani, Lillani.

Lena: Although a diminutive of Helen, this name is also used independently.

Leona: Feminine version of the Latin name Leo, 'the lion', honouring the king of the beasts. Also Leonie, Leonella.

Leonora: A form of Eleanor, which in turn is a form of Helen. See Nora.

Lesley: This name means 'from the gray stronghold' and is the feminine form of the Celtic name Leslie. This was used only as a surname but became popular as a first name for boys and girls in the late nineteenth century. Today's parents could use either spelling for either sex!

Letitia: A Latin name which sounds like a sneeze and means 'gladness'. This name was taken from the Romans by the English in the form of Lettice. The Italian is Letizia, and English pet forms are Letty, Leta and Tish.

Letty: See Alethea and Letitia.

Lewanna: 'As pure as the white moon' is the meaning of this Hebrew name.

Lexie: See Alexandra.

Liana: From the French *lier* meaning 'to bind', this flower name is in honour of the climbing tropical plant. Also a variation of Leanne.

Libby: See Elizabeth.

Lida: This name of Slavonic origin means 'loved by all'.

Lila: See Delilah.

Lilith: Of Assyrian-Babylonian origin, meaning 'storm-demon' in Jewish folklore.

Lillian: From the Latin for lily, this is one of the oldest of the flower names and is a Christian icon of purity.

Lily is the popular pet form, and among the many English variations are Lilah, Lilia, Lilianna, Lilicia, Lillis, Lilyan. The French-Latin modern combination name meaning 'beautiful lily' is Lilybelle, and Lilyanne is the Greek-Hebrew modern combination form.

Australia's first woman police officer was Lillian May Armfield, 1884–1971.

Lina: Considered an independent name, this is also a German diminutive of Carolina, as well as the English diminutive of Adelina and Evelina.

Linda/Lindy: This name comes from the Old German word *lindi*, meaning 'serpent'; the Spanish meaning is 'pretty or beautiful one'. A popular independent name, it is also a shortened form of Melinda. See also Lindy-Lou.

Lindsay/Lyndsay: This Anglo-Saxon name means 'pool island', and can be used for girls and boys.

Lindy: See Melinda.

Lindy-Lou: A Latin-German combined name meaning 'beautiful, famed warrior-maid'. This popular name combines the shortened forms of Linda and Louise.

Linette: See Lynette.

Lisa: Although a form of Elizabeth, this has become a very popular independent name. Also Lisette, Liza.

Lisette: See Lisa and Elizabeth.

Liza: See Lisa and Elizabeth.

Lois: An old Greek name meaning 'the better', this became a popular Puritan name as it signifies virtue.

Lola: Considered an independent name, this is actually a diminutive of the Spanish name Dolores. Lola Montez was the stage name of the Irish dancer, Maria Dolores Eliza Rosanna Gilbert, sometime mistress of Louis I of Bavaria and later visitor to the Victorian goldfields. The diminutive form is Lolita.

Lori: See Laura.

Loris: See Laura.

Lorna: R. D. Blackmore created this name for his best-selling novel *Lorna Doone* (1869).

Lorraine: French, meaning 'famous in battle'. Also Loraine.

✗ *Louise:* An ever-popular name which is the feminine form of the Latin boy's name Aloysius. There are many shortened, combined and pet forms including Cindy-Lou, Eloisa, Eloise, Heloise, Lindy-Lou, Lou, Louisa, Lulu, Marylou.

Lucinda: See Lucy.

Lucy: From the Latin for 'light', in Roman times it was often given to babies born at dawn. Among the many variations also considered fashionable today are Lucia, Lucille, Lucinda, Cindy.

Lurline: The origin is Teutonic and the meaning is 'the alluring'!

Lycia: See Alice.

Lydia: Lydia was a rich trading country in ancient Asia Minor where the women were renowned for their beauty. Also Lidia, Lidie, Lydie.

Lynette: From the Latin, meaning 'the flax'. Tennyson made the name popular with his Arthurian romance between Lynette and Gareth in *Idylls of the King*. Other forms are Linnet, Linette, Lyn, Lynne.

Lynda: See Linda.

M

Mabel: Derived from the Latin word *amabilis*, meaning 'lovable'. A popular Victorian name, made less popular by the radio program 'Dad and Dave'.

Madeline: Taken from the birthplace of St Mary Magdalene, the French version Madeleine has long been popular. Variations are Madelaine, Madalyn, Madelena, Magda, Magdala, Magdalene, Magdelena. See also Marlene.

Maeve: This is an anglicised version of Meadhbh who was a first-century Irish queen. Still a popular

Irish name in the modern form, also as Mave and Meave.

Magnolia: One of the Latin flower names. Shortened forms are Maggie, Nola and Nolie.

Maida: An Anglo-Saxon name meaning 'the maiden', which along with Maidie was popular during Victorian and Edwardian times.

Malvina: Feminine of the Teutonic name Melvin meaning 'chieftain'. Also Malvinia, Melva and Melvina and pet forms Mallie and Mellie.

Manuela: The Spanish feminine of Manuel, meaning 'God with us'. The diminutive is Manuelita.

Marah: Meaning 'bitter', this was the original Hebrew form of Mary.

Marcella: Feminine version of the Latin Mark, and meaning 'belonging to Mars', the god of war.

Marcella and Marcia were names given to daughters of the powerful Roman family of Marcus. These names were later used by Christians in honour of St Mark.

Other variations are Marcelle, Marcellina, Marcie, Marsha.

Marcia: See Marcella.

Margaret: Probably from the Latin for pearl.

Many European queens and princesses bore this name, the first-known English royal Margaret being the daughter of Henry III. The sister of Queen Elizabeth was named Margaret Rose in 1930, causing a revival in the name's popularity. Megan, the Welsh pet-form from Meg, is widely used today.

Other forms are Margareta, Margaretta, Margarita, Margery, Margherita, Margot, Marguerite, Marjorie. The most usual pet forms are Greta, Madge, Maggie, Maisie, May, Meg, Meta, Peg, Peggy, and Rita.

Margery: Although this is a variation of Margaret it is now considered an independent name from the French Marguerite. Marjorie is the favoured Scottish spelling. See Margaret.

Marghorita: See Margaret and Rita.

Margot: Also adapted from Marguerite, Margot has become an independent name through common usage in the past. See Margaret.

Maria: See Mary and Ria.

Marian: See Ann(e) and Mary.

Maribelle: A combination of Mary and Belle or Bella, thus meaning 'beautiful Mary'. Also Marabelle, Maribel, Maribella, Marybelle.

Marie: See Mary.

Marietta: An American name which originated from Marietta, Ohio, a town called after the French Queen Marie Antoinette.

Marigold: A pretty English flower name for the plant originally called 'Mary's gold'.

Marilla: Used by L. M. Montgomery in her books about Anne of Green Gables.

Marilyn: An American version of Mary.

Marina: Latin, meaning 'of the sea'. Always a favoured name of European Catholic families, it became popular in England during the 1930s when

Princess Marina married the Duke of Kent.

Marion: A 'Mary' name brought to England by the Normans and made popular by Robin Hood's friend, Maid Marion.

Marjorie: See Margery.

Marlene: In Hebrew 'the elevated', and also considered to be a contraction of Madeline. Marlene Dietrich brought fame, popularity and mystique to this name. Also Marleen, Marlina.

Marsha: See Marcella.

Martha: Aramaic for 'of the household'. The biblical Martha, sister of Mary Magdalene, friend of Jesus, was the supreme example of housewifely virtue. Also Marta and Matty.

Martina: The feminine of Martin, Martina means 'war-like', as Martina Navratilova's opponents would appreciate. The French version, Martine, is also popular. Tina is the short version.

Mary: This most common of feminine first names has an obscure background, and the origins suggested are many. It has been claimed to be an ancient Egyptian name, 'meri Amen' meaning 'beloved of Amen', an Egyptian god of 1700 BC. However, it seems acceptable to believe that Mary came from Miriam, mentioned in the Book of Exodus, and sister of Moses and Aaron. After 1100 when the Crusaders returned from the Holy Land Mary became the most consistently used name in Europe: in Spain and Italy as Maria, in France as Marie, in Wales as Mair and Maire, and Moira or Maureen in

Ireland. Mimi, Minnie, Mitzi, Molly and Polly are terms of endearment from Mary. See also Ann(e), Marah, Maribelle, May and Ria.
Marylou: A modern name combining Mary and Louise.
Matilda: An Old High German name meaning 'mighty battlemaid'. A favourite name after the Norman invasion and borne by the wife of William the Conqueror. William's granddaughter was also Matilda, but was commonly known as Maud, the common form of Matilda. Also Mathilda, Matty, Maud, Maude, Tilly.
Maud(e): See Matilda.
Maureen: Another derivation of Mary, this is from Ireland where, along with Maire, it is commonly used. The pet form of Mo became popular with tennis champ 'Little Mo' Connelly.
Mavis: An Old French name meaning 'the song thrush'. More popular with poets than twentieth-century parents.
Maxine: From the French masculine Maximilian, 'the greatest'. Also Max, Maxie, Maxima, Maxime.
May: The Romans named their spring month after Maia their Earth Mother, who was the goddess-wife of Vulcan. May is also another form of Margaret or Mary.
Meg: See Margaret.
Megan: Welsh, meaning 'the strong'. Also a derivation of Margaret, from Meg.
Melanie: Of Greek origin, meaning 'dark' or 'black'.

In Greek mythology Demeter (or Melania, the earth goddess) wore black all winter until her daughter Persephone returned bringing the spring. The English first used the Italian form Melania, then adopted the French Melanie.

Margaret Mitchell's book *Gone with the Wind* popularised this name. A popular name in Australia, particularly during the 1970s.

Melba: Old English feminine form of Melbourne, meaning 'from the mill stream'. Dame Nellie chose this in honour of her home town.

Melina: See Carmel.

Melinda: A Greek name meaning 'mild and gentle', this name is a popular one of the seventies and eighties. Lindy is the pet form. See also Linda.

Melissa: Feminine of the Greek masculine name Melitus, meaning 'honey' or 'honey-bee'. Melissa through the ages has been the heroine of Italian legend, Babylonian mythology, German and English literature, and is popular today. Other forms are Lissa, Mel, Melita, Melitta, Misha, Missy.

Melody: From the Greek *melos*, 'a song' and, literally, 'melody', a name with a ring to it!

Meredith: A Celtic name meaning 'protector of the sea'. Also Merry.

Meryl: A Latin name meaning 'blackbird'. Also Merrill.

Meta: From the Latin, meaning 'ambition' or 'goal', and also a diminutive of Margaret.

Mia: Romantic Italian/Spanish name meaning

'mine'. A short and sweet first name to use with a multi-syllabic second name.

Michelle: French feminine version of the Hebrew Michael, meaning 'like God'. Especially popular in the sixties with the Beatles' 'Michelle'. Also Michaela, Michaelina, Mikaela.

Mignon: French, meaning 'delicate, dainty, graceful and petite'.

Mildred: An Anglo-Saxon name which literally means 'mild power'. This name was popular under the Hanoverians and again with the Victorians, who favoured medieval names. Also Millie, Milly.

Millicent: This Teutonic name means 'strong worker' or 'energetic'.

Millie/Milly: Diminutives of Amelia, Camille, Mildred and Millicent.

Mirabel: 'Admired for her beauty' is the Latin meaning of this name, which is often shortened to Belle. Also Mirabelle.

Miranda: A Latin name meaning 'greatly admired'. Shakespeare introduced this name to England through the heroine of *The Tempest*. Joan Lindsay used the name Miranda for the ethereal schoolgirl who disappeared in the story *Picnic at Hanging Rock*.

Miriam: Hebrew name from which Mary possibly originated. See Mary.

Misha: See Melissa.

Mitzi: See Mary.

Moira: See Mary.

Molly: See Mary.

Mona: See Shimona.

Monica: From the Latin *monere*, 'to advise or warn'. This name is used widely today in the French form, Monique.

Monique: See Monica.

Morgan: Feminine and masculine Welsh name meaning 'from the sea shore'. Also Morgana.

Muriel: A Celtic name meaning 'sparkling sea' which regained popularity during the Victorian era.

Myfanwy: This Welsh name meaning 'my fine one' has always been popular in Wales. Also Myvanwy.

N

Nadia: Slavic meaning 'hope'. Also popular in the French form Nadine.

Nan/Nanette: See Nancy.

Nancy: This name, along with Nan and Nanette, is considered a variation of Anne and Hannah.

Naomi: 'Pleasant one' is the meaning of this Hebrew name favoured by the Puritans. The Biblical Naomi was the faithful friend and mother-in-law of Ruth.

Narelle: See Helen.

Natalie: From the Latin *natalis*, 'natal, or birth day', this is a popular name especially for Christmas babies. The Russian is Natasha, the French Noelle, and other forms are Natalia, and Nathalie.

Natasha: See Natalie.

Nell/Nellie: See Helen.

Neoma: A Greek name meaning 'the new moon'. The ancient Greek festival Neomania was a celebration of the new moon, and Neoma became a popular name for girls born at that time.

Nerida: Aboriginal name which means 'a flower'.

Nerilee: See Nerolie.

Nerine: Feminine of the Latin Nereus, meaning 'of the sea'. Greek myths tell of beautiful girls called Nereids, or nymphs, who lived near the sea. Shakespeare introduced the variation Nerissa, Portia's servant. Also Nerita, Nerice.

Nerolie: Italian feminine version of Nero, meaning 'the black'. Neroli, the brown oil distilled from orange-tree flowers for use in perfume, was named after the Italian princess who discovered it. Also Nerilee.

Nessie: See Agnes.

Netta: Latin, meaning 'pure and neat'. Also used as the diminutive of Antoinette, Jeanette and Henrietta. Also Netti, Netty.

Ngaio: Maori name, meaning 'a tree'.

Ngaire: Maori name for flax, which is also written as Nyree.

Nicola: Feminine of the Greek Nicholas, meaning 'the people's victory', sometimes given as a Christmas name in honour of St Nicholas of Russia. Popular in this form and also in the French Nicole and Nicolette. The Greek variation is Nicolina, and the pet form is Nicky.

Nicolette: See Collette.
Nina: Spanish word for 'little girl', and short form of the Russian name Annina. Also Nena, Ninetta, Ninette.
Nissa: This Scandinavian name is for 'friendly elf' – a fairy who can only be seen by lovers.
Noelle: French name popular for Christmas babies. See Natalie.
Nola: Celtic name for 'the noble', and also a diminutive of Olivia and Magnolia.
Nona: A Latin name for 'the ninth'. This was a favourite Italian name for the ninth-born, not so common these days! It can also be a pet-name for grandmother.
Nora: Irish version of Eleanor, Honora, Helen or Leonora.
Norma: Latin name meaning, as it suggests, 'the norm', popular in the 1930s and 40s.
Nyree: See Ngaire.

O

Obelia: A Greek name related to obelisk (pillar).
Octavia: Feminine of the Latin Octavius, 'the eighth'. This name came from the Octavian family of Rome and was given to the eighth child.
Odessa: Greek, meaning 'of the Odyssey', and a place name for the city in Russia.

Odette: French for 'home lover', the good woman who makes a house a home.

Olga: A Teutonic name for 'one who has been anointed in the service of God'.

x ***Olivia:*** Latin for 'the olive', the symbol of peace. A popular name today, and well known because of the singer Olivia Newton-John who was born in England, educated in Australia and lives in America. Also Olive, Livia, Livvy, Nola, Nollie.

Olwen: Welsh, meaning 'white footprint', from a legend that white herbs sprang up wherever Olwen, the giantess, trod. Also Olwyn.

Olympia: Mythology tells of Mt Olympus in Macedonia, the resting place of the gods.

Ona/Oona: See Una.

Oneida: American-Indian name, meaning 'the awaited'.

Oonah: See Una.

Ophelia: Greek, meaning 'a serpent', considered a symbol of invincibility and wisdom. This name was popular in medieval times and again during the Victorian era.

Ora: See Aurora.

Orsa/Orsola: See Ursula.

P

Paloma: Spanish name meaning 'the dove', chosen by painter Pablo Picasso for his daughter.

Pamela: Another literary coinage.

The writer Samuel Richardson used this name for the main character of his novel *Pamela, or Virtue Rewarded* in 1740. Also a popular choice of parents in the 1930s and 40s.

Pandora: In Greek mythology Pandora was the first woman, created by Zeus as his revenge on man and Prometheus who had stolen fire from heaven. Zeus gave Pandora a box which he forbade her to open. She disobeyed, letting out all the evils of the world, but hope remained.

Pansy: 'Fragrant', from the Greek.

Patience: Latin, meaning 'endurance', adopted by the English Puritans.

Patricia: The Patricians of Ancient Rome were essentially the nobles. The name was popularised in modern times by Princess Patricia of Connaught, Queen Victoria's granddaughter, who was known as Pat.

Other forms are Patsy, Patty, Pattie, Tish and Tricia. Patrizia is a favourite Italian name.

Paula: Feminine of the Latin Paul, meaning 'small'. Paula and Pauline were popular Australian names during the 1950s, with Pol as a pet form.

Pauline: See Paula.

Pearl: This jewel name, like Ruby and Crystal, was popular in the Edwardian era.

Peg/Peggy: See Margaret.

Penelope: Greek for 'the weaver', and a symbol of wifely fidelity.

Penelope, wife of Ulysses, had many would-be suitors during her husband's ten-year absence fighting the Trojan War. Penelope refused to remarry until her tapestry was completed and, believing Ulysses would return, unravelled each night what she had woven that day.

Also Penne, Penny, Pen.

Petra: Feminine of the Greek Peter, 'a rock'. Also Petrea, Petrina, Petronella, Petronia, Pierella, Pierette.

Petunia: Indian name for the flower.

Philippa: Greek, meaning 'lover of horses', making it suitable for many Australian girls. Pip and Pippa are the pet forms.

Philomena: The Greek nightingale who sings to the moon.

Phoebe: To the ancient Greeks Phoebus was the sun god and Phoebe goddess of the moon.

Phyllis: Greek, meaning 'green bough'. Also Fillis, Phillida, Phyllida.

Pia: A Latin name meaning 'devout'.

Polly: A pet name from Mary, or possibly from a Flemish usage for 'girl'. Developed into the optimist of children's books, Pollyanna.

Poppy: The flower which symbolises peace (from the Latin). A popular name during Victorian times it is becoming fashionable again.

Primrose: Latin flower name meaning 'the first rose', this is another fashionable name of Victorian times. Also Prunella, Primmie, Rose, Rosa.

Priscilla: Latin, meaning 'the primitive or ancient'. Other forms are Prissie and Cilla.

Prudence: Latin, meaning 'discretion', and another of the Puritan virtue names which are hard to live up to! Popular today, especially in the short form, Prue.

Prunella: A French name for the sloe plum or prunus. See Primrose.

Q

Queenie: This was often used as a nickname for girls christened Victoria in the days of the great English queen.

Querida: Spanish, meaning beloved, and more often used as an endearment than as a given name.

R

Rachel: This Hebrew name means 'ewe', and symbolises innocence. The biblical Rachel was Jacob's wife. Also Rachelle, Rochelle, Raquel, Rae, Shelley.

Rae: See Rachel.

Ramona: The female form of the Teutonic name Raymond, meaning 'protective judgement'.

Rani: Sanskrit, meaning 'a princess'.

Raquel: See Rachel.

Rebecca: The Hebrew origin of 'binding together' suggested the compliant wife, as was Rebecca in the Bible, to Isaac. It later became a widely used name among the Puritans both in England and the Americas, and has become very popular again.

The diminutive is Becky.

Regina: From the Latin for 'queen' as in *Regina Caeli*, queen of heaven. Other forms are Raina, Reina, Reyna and Regan.

Renata: From the Latin, 'born again', it is Renata in German, René or Renée in French.

René(e): See Renata.

Rhea: Greek for 'poppy'. In Greek mythology she was the mother of all gods.

Rhiannon: This lovely Welsh name means 'nymph'.

Rhoda: Greek for 'rose'.

Ria: This Spanish name means 'the river'. It is also a diminutive of Maria and Mary.

Rita: This Sanskrit name means 'order' or 'law'; it is also a diminutive of Margherita 'a pearl'. To Beatles fans, Rita will always be the lovely meter maid.

Roberta: The feminine of Robert, this is an old German name which means 'bright fame'. Also Robin, Robyn, Robina, Robinetta, Bobbie.

Robina: See Roberta.

Robyn: See Roberta.

Rochella: Feminine of the Latin Roche, hence 'little rock'. Also Rochelle and Rochette.

Rohana: Sanskrit, meaning 'sandalwood tree', the aromatic wood used for carving, burned as incense, and which yields fragrant oil for perfume.

Rosa: See Rose.

Rose: The Latin form of the flower name has also given Rosa, Roseanna, Roseanne, Rosina, Rosita, Rosie, Rosaleen, Rho, Rosalinda, Rosamond, Rosamund, Rosemary, Ros and Roslyn.

Rosemary: This is a combination of Rose and Mary, but traces back to the Latin, meaning 'dew of the sea'. It is also a plant name, for the herb of remembrance.

Rowena: Celtic, meaning 'white-maned'. Rowena was a legendary Saxon princess of ancient Britain. A popular name after Sir Walter Scott's heroine in his novel *Ivanhoe*.

Roxanna: A Persian name meaning 'brilliant'. Also Roxanne. The pet forms of Rox, Roxie or Roxy are also popular.

Ruby: One of the jewel names popular with the Edwardians.

Ruth: Hebrew, probably meaning 'friend'. The biblical Ruth became a symbol of devotion and loyalty when she followed her husband into exile. Her name was a favourite with the Puritans.

S

Sabina: The Sabines were an ancient Italian people conquered by the Romans in 290 BC and made famous by literary and artistic depictions of 'The Rape of the Sabine Women'.

Sabrina: In Latin, a princess.

Sally: Originally a pet form of Sarah, but now considered an independent name meaning 'princess'.

Samantha: Aramaic for 'listener', and a biblical name which was revived late last century. Particularly popular in Australia after Grace Kelly played Samantha in the film *High Society*.

Sandra: A diminutive form of Alexandra, through the Italian Alessandra meaning 'protector'. One of the popular baby-boomer names, there are many Mums of today's teenagers who answer to Sandy.

Sarah: A Hebrew name meaning 'princess'. Abraham's wife was originally Sarai before Jehovah changed this name to Sarah. Often the 'h' is dropped to give Sara, and other variations are Sade, Sadie, Saida, Sally, Sari, Sarine, Sarita, Sayda, Zadah, Zara, Zarah.

Scarlett: Middle English, meaning 'a rich red cloth'. Originally this was a surname, probably that of a cloth-trader. A famous first name through the heroine of Margaret Mitchell's *Gone with the Wind*, Scarlett O'Hara.

Selena: Selene was the moon goddess in Greek mythology. Also Celie, Celina, Celinda, Selina.

Seraphina: Feminine of the Hebrew Seraph, 'the enthusiastic believer', Serafina is a popular Italian name and is often shortened to Fina.

Serena: Feminine form of the Latin for 'tranquil'.

Shaina: A Yiddish name which means 'beautiful'.

Shane: Masculine or feminine, this is a form of John or Jane.

At the Munich Olympic Games in 1972 Shane Gould won the 200 and 400 metres women's freestyle and the 200 metres individual medley, each in new Olympic and world record time.

Shani: African, meaning 'wonderful'.

Shannon: Feminine and masculine Celtic, meaning 'slow waters'.

Shantelle: See Chantal.

Sharon: Hebrew, meaning 'the plain', this is the fertile plain between Jaffa and Mt Carmel in Israel.

Sheena: An Anglicised form of the Gaelic Sine, a form of Jane or Jean. Other forms are Sheenah and Shena.

Sheila: A very popular Irish name derived from Cecilia and which has become a crude generic for Australian women. Also Sheelagh, Sheilah, Shelagh.

Shelley: Anglo-Saxon, meaning 'from the edge of the meadow', this was often given to boys as well as girls in honour of the poet Percy Bysshe Shelley. See also Rachel.

Sheryl: See Cheryl.

Shimona: Hebrew for 'little princess', it is often reduced to the short form, Mona.

Shirley: Old English, meaning 'the shining meadow', this was popular during the 1930s because of the precocious singing/dancing/smiling child-star, Shirley Temple. Also Shirlee, Shirleen, Shirlene, Shirlie.

Shona: A form of Jane with Celtic origins.

Sibil: In ancient Greece the Sibyls were prophets. Also Sibella, Sibilla or Sybilla.

Sidra: Latin name, meaning 'of the stars'.

Sigrid: Old Norse for 'victory ride'. Popular in Scandinavia and well known here through the actress Sigrid Thornton.

Silvana: See Sylvia.

Simone: Feminine version of Simon. Also Simona, Simonette.

Siobhán: Irish for Jane, and pronounced 'Shoo-vawn' (with the accent on the second syllable).

Sirena: This means 'sweet singer' or siren', and comes from the Greek myth of the sirens whose songs lured sailors to their deaths.

Sissie: See Cecilia.

Sofia: See Sophia.

Sonia: This Russian form of Sophie often appears as Sonja. See Sophia.

Sophia: This is the Greek word for 'wisdom'. St Sophia was the wise mother of the three daughters, Faith, Hope and Charity. The shorter version, Sophie, is fashionable today. Also Sofia, Sonia.

Stacie/Stacy: See Anastasia.

Steffie: See Stephanie.

Stella: Latin for 'star', this name became popular for Catholic girls because Stella Maris, star of the sea, is a name for the Virgin Mary. See also Esther.

Stephanie: Feminine of the Greek Stephen, meaning 'crown'. Also Steffie, Stephana, Stevana, Stevania, Stevena, Stevie.

Susan: Hebrew flower name meaning 'lily'.

A popular name during the baby-boomer years, Australia's schools were also full of Susans and Suzannes during the 1950s and 60s. Also Su, Sue, Suke, Sukey, Sukie, Susanna, Susannah, Suse, Susie, Susy, Suzanna, Suzanne, Suze, Suzette, Suzie.

Sybil: See Sibyl.

Sylvia: Of Latin origin, for one who lives in the forest, Sylvia has been poetically popular in pastorals. Also Silvia and Silvana.

T

Tabitha: Aramaic for 'gazelle'.

Tamara: From the Hebrew Tamar, 'a palm tree'. The shorter form of Tammy/Tammie is a popular variation.

Tamsin: From Thomasina, feminine of Thomas, meaning 'twin'. A girl/boy pair of twins could be called Tamsin and Thomas or Tammy and Tommy!

Tania: The abbreviated form of the Russian Titania, 'the fairy queen'. Also Tanya. See Titania.

Tansy: Latin for 'tenacious', and name for the yellow-flowered herb.

Tanya: See Tania.

Tara: Gaelic, meaning 'crag' or 'tower', and place name in honour of the Irish city.

Tatum: Feminine form of the Anglo-Saxon Tate, 'cheerful'.

Terry: See Theresa.

Tessa: Greek, meaning 'the fourth', and a name for daughter number four. Also a variation of Theresa.

Thalia: Meaning 'blooming', in Greek mythology Thalia was the muse of poetry and comedy. Tahlia.

Thea: Greek word for 'goddess', this name is also the diminutive of Althea and Dorothea.

Theodora: See Dorothy.

Theresa: Latin for 'to harvest'.

One of the earliest bearers of this name was St

Therasia who lived in Spain during the fifth century. The name then spread throughout the Roman Catholic world during the sixteenth century after St Theresa of Avila. Also Teresa, Terese, Terry, Tessa, Tracy, Tressa.

Thomasina: See Tamsin.

Thora: Feminine of the Norse God Thor, 'the thunderer'.

Tiffany: Pet form of the Greek Theophania, 'when God was made known'. Also Tiffanie, Tiffie, Tiffy.

Tina: Originally short for Clementina, it has become a diminutive for many names such as Bettina, Christina, Martina, Valentina, and an independent name in its own right.

Tish: See Letitia and Patricia.

Titania: Derived from mythological giants, the Titans of Greece. Also Tania and Tanya.

Toni: See Antonia.

Topaz: Greek jewel name for the precious yellow stone.

Tourmaline: Another jewel name, of Sri Lankan origin.

Tracy: Anglo-Saxon name for 'the brave', and a form of Theresa. This has been a popular girl's name since the 1960s. Also Tracey.

Trixie: See Beatrice.

Trudy: Teutonic for 'loved one', and a diminutive of Gertrude.

U

Ultima: Latin for 'the ultimate, or last' and obviously the name given to the last daughter of a large family.

Una: From the Latin *unus*, meaning 'one'. The Puritans adopted the name Unity as one of their virtue names. The popular Irish version is Oonagh. Also Ona, Oona.

Undine: In Roman mythology Undine was the water sprite who fell in love with a mortal.

Unity: See Una.

Ursula: From the Latin Ursus, 'bear'. Also Orsa, Orsola, Ursel, Ursola, Ursulette.

V

Valda: From the Teutonic suggesting a warrior.

Valentina: Valentine is the patron saint of lovers, thus St Valentine's Day. The diminutives are Val and Tina.

Valerie: From the name of an old Roman family, so distinguished that they had special seats in the Colosseum. The diminutive is Val.

Valma: The Welsh name for a mayflower. Also Valmai.

Vanessa: A Greek name meaning 'butterfly'. Also Vanny, Vann, Van and Phanessa.

Vashti: A name of Persian origin which means 'beautiful'.

Velda: From the Teutonic Veleda, 'a wise person'.

Venus: The goddess of love. Other forms are Venice, Venetia, Venita.

Vera: From the Latin for 'truth'. A popular name during World War II when Vera Lynn, sweetheart of the troops, was singing about Dover's white cliffs. Diminutive of Veronica. Also Verity.

Verity: See Vera.

Veronica: 'True image', in honour of St Veronica, who wiped Christ's face as he carried the cross to Calvary. Because his image remained on her cloth she was made the patron saint of photographers. Nicky, Ronnie and Vera are short variations.

Vicki: See Victoria.

Victoria: From the Latin 'victorious'. Made popular by the long reign of Queen Victoria over the British Empire from 1837 to 1901. Also Vicki, Vicky.

Vida: The feminine form of David, and contraction of the Welsh Davida.

Violet: A flower name from the Latin, popular in Scotland.

Also Violette, Yolette, Yolande, Viola, Joletta, Yolante, Yolanthe and Yolanda.

Virginia: From the Roman family name of Virginius. Also Virgilia, Ginger, Ginnie.

Vivian: A name used for both sexes with Vivian being

the favoured boy's spelling and Vivien for girls. From the Latin for 'alive'. Other forms are Viviana, Vivienne, Vyvyan, Vyvian and Viv.

W

Wanda: A Teutonic name from Wendla, 'the wanderer'. Also Wandis, Wendelin, Wendeline, Wenda, Wendy.
Wendy: The implied meaning is 'friend' from the heroine in J M Barrie's play *'Peter Pan'*. Also a diminutive of Gwendoline and Wanda.
Wenonah: An American-Indian name meaning 'first born', which Longfellow used in 'Hiawatha'. Also Wenona, Winona.
Wilhelmina: Old High German feminine version of Wilhelm or William. Also Willa, Wilma, Velma, Willy, Willie, Minny, Mina.
Winifred: Teutonic name meaning 'peaceful friend'.
Wynne: A Celtic name meaning 'fair'.

X

Xanthe: Greek, meaning golden or yellow-haired.
Xaviera: Feminine of Xavier.
Xylia: A Greek name akin to Silvia.

Y

Yasmine: The alternative spelling for Jasmine.
Yedda: Teutonic for 'the singer'.
Yetta: Anglo-Saxon for 'the given'. Also a diminutive of Henrietta.
Yoko: Meaning 'determined woman', this Japanese name became well known in the west through Mrs John Lennon, Yoko Ono.
Yolande: French form of the flower name Violet.
Yoorala: Aboriginal, meaning 'affection'.
Yoorana: Another Aboriginal name, this one meaning 'loving'.
Yoshi: Japanese name meaning respectful.
Yvonne: French feminine of the Scandinavian Yves or Iver, 'the archer', a great name for a live-wire Sagittarian. Also Evonne, Yvette, Vonnie.

Z

Zada: An Arabic name meaning prosperous. Also Zadah.
Zandra: Another spelling of Sandra.
Zane: See Jane.
Zara: This form of Sarah made popular in Australia by Dame Zara Holt, was given a further boost in

1981 when Princess Anne named her daughter Zara Anne Elizabeth.

Zerlinda: A Hebrew name meaning 'beautiful as the dawn'. Also Zerlina.

Zillah: Hebrew, meaning 'shade'. Also Zilla.

Zoe: A Greek name meaning 'life', the equivalent of the Hebrew name, Eve.

Zuleika: Arabic, meaning 'the fair'.

BOYS

A

Aaron: Of Hebrew origin meaning 'high mountain'. In the Old Testament Aaron was the older brother of Moses. Other forms are Aharon, Haroun.

Abel: Hebrew for 'the breath'. The biblical Abel was the second son of Adam and Eve and was killed by his brother, Cain. Somehow the diminutive form Nab evolved from this. Also Abell, Able and the Hebrew, Hebel.

Abner: Hebrew for 'father of light'. In the Bible Abner was commander-in-chief of the army of Saul, who waged war against King David.

Abraham: Hebrew name meaning 'father of multitudes'. Abraham was the first patriarch.

The original form was Abram which, with Bram, was introduced to New Amsterdam (New York) by the Dutch. A popular name in America.

Also Abie, Abira, Aby, Abe, Arum, Ibrahim.

Absalom: 'Father of peace' in Hebrew, Absalom in the Bible was the favourite, albeit rebellious, son of King David.

Ace: This Latin name means 'unity, or the unit' and implies 'one who excels'.

Adam: Hebrew, meaning 'of the red earth' from which God formed the first man. The Hebrews and Romans seemed to make little use of this old name, leaving it to the Celts to popularise it.

As Adams (Adam's son), this became a common family name and the basis for many other surnames. Today a popular boy's name, especially for a first son.

Adrian: From the Latin for 'of Adria', originally from *ater* 'the black'. Adria was a seaport which also gave its name to the Adriatic Sea.

The form Hadrian was adopted when the Roman Emperor, Hadrianus, built his wall across Northern England.

Aidan: Of Celtic origin, this name means 'little fiery one', and honours the Irish St Aidan, Edan or Egan.

Aiken: An Anglo-Saxon name meaning 'the oaken' for the oak tree which in Ancient England was a symbol of strength.

Ainsley: This Anglo-Saxon name means 'Ain's meadow'. Ain was the original form of Ann and a place name in England. Ann was once a masculine as well as feminine name. Also Ainslie.

Alan: Meaning 'harmony', which has been used in many forms through the centuries, the first known bearer of this name was Alawn, a Celtic poet of the first century AD. Other recorded ancient forms are Eilian, Ailin, Alun and Alon. Alan and Allan are the usual forms today, with Allen being the most accepted spelling of the surname.

Alastair: See Alexander.

Alaster/Alister: See Alexander.

Albert: This Teutonic name meaning 'illustrious through nobility', originated as Albrecht or

Adelbrecht, and began in England as Ethelbert, Adalbert or Adelbert.

The name was a common one for Austro-Hungarian nobility and gained popularity in Britain at the time of Queen Victoria's marriage to Prince Albert of Saxony in 1840.

Bert is the common abbreviation, not often heard today, though we all know Albert Watson Newton, star of radio and television.

Alexander: From the Greek meaning 'protector of mankind'. This became a name of heroic proportions through Alexander the Great, King of Macedon, who gave the name to several cities.

Other famous Alexanders have included kings, emperors, czars, saints and eight popes. Many different forms of this old name have evolved, among them Alasdair, Alastair, Alec, Aleck, Alex, Alexis, Alick, Allister.

Alfred: Anglo-Saxon meaning 'the wise counsel of the elf'.

Alfred the Great (849-99) the King of Wessex, excelled as a statesman, a soldier and a scholar, and was the most famous bearer of this name.

Also Alfie, Alf and Al.

Allan/Allen: See Alan.

Allister: See Alexander.

Algernon: This French name developed in the eleventh century for the Count of Boulogne, who was distinguished from his father by the fact that he had a moustache and was known as Eustace *aux* *gernons* which meant 'with the whiskers' in Norman French.

Aloysius: Meaning 'the Son of Louis' from the French, Aloysius, the Latin version has come into popular usage after the young Italian Jesuit, St Aloysius Gonzaga.

Alphonse: Of Teutonic origin meaning 'noble and ready for battle', this was the name given to many Portuguese and Spanish kings in the forms Alfonso or Alonso. Other forms are Alphonso, Alonzo, Lonny and Lon.

Alton: An Anglo-Saxon name which means 'dweller in the old town'.

Alvin: Teutonic name which means 'friend of all' or 'noble friend'. The Anglo-Saxon meaning became 'elf friend'. See Elvin.

Andrew: Greek, meaning 'strong or manly', this is one of the most consistently popular boys' names. The biblical Andrew was Christ's first disciple, and later the patron saint of Scotland.

Other forms are Andy and Drew; the Greek is Andreas, the Italian is Andrea, and the French is André.

Angus: One of the best-loved of all Scottish names, originally from Aonghus, meaning 'unique choice'.

The first known bearer of this name is Aonghus Turimleach, who in the third century BC invaded Scotland from his homeland of Ireland. Still a popular name, especially in the short form of Gus.

Anthony/Antony: Latin name meaning 'inestimable' or 'priceless'. Historically, a famous bearer of this name was Caesar's close friend and Cleopatra's lover, Mark Antony.

This name became a favourite of the Christian world through St Anthony of Padua, patron saint of little children and of Italy. Tony is the pet form.

The French Antoine and the Italian Antonio and Tonio are popular in those languages.

Archibald: German, meaning 'noble and truly bold', this old name was a favourite of Teutonic warriors.

Arian: Greek name meaning 'of Ares', Ares being the god of war. Also Arius, Arianus.

Aries: In Latin 'a ram', and the Greek for 'a young kid', this is a sign of the zodiac.

Aristotle: Still a popular Greek name which means 'best of the thinkers'.

Armstrong: Anglo-Saxon name meaning 'strong arm' for the tough warrior who could swing a battle-axe, or for today's arm-wrestler!

Arnold: This Teutonic name means 'powerful eagle', and was introduced to Britain by the Normans as Arnaud. Other forms are Arnie, Arny, Arent.

Arthur: Celtic name meaning 'strong as a bear'. The legendary King Arthur has kept this name in vogue, popular after Queen Victoria named her third son Arthur. Also Art and Arty.

Asher: A Hebrew name meaning 'happy one' or 'laughing one'. In biblical history Asher was a son of

Jacob and his descendants in Palestine were known as Asherites.

Ashley: Old English name which means 'from the ash-tree lea, or meadow'. A popular name in this form for a boy, and as Ashleigh for a girl.

Also Ashford.

Augustus: From the Latin, meaning 'high, honoured' or 'mighty', this title was carried by many Roman emperors. Also August and Augustine, with the short form Gus.

B

Baldwin: From the Old German meaning 'bold protector', this name arrived in Flanders in the Middle Ages and also acquired a Welsh form, Maldwyn.

Barnaby: Aramaic for 'son of exhortation', this name implies that prayers have been answered, presumably for a son. The short variation is Barney or Barnie.

Barry: An Old Celtic name meaning 'fine marksman' which originated from Bearach and was almost exclusively Irish until the nineteenth century.

One of Australia's best-known Barrys is John Barry Humphries, constant companion of Dame Edna Everage. Also Barrie (and Bazza!).

Bartholomew: This is Hebrew and means 'son of Talmai' – 'son of furrows, ploughman'. Barthol, Barth, Bart and Bat are short forms.

Basil: Greek, meaning 'the kingly, royal'. Well known today because of Basil Fawlty, and the sweet herb, basil.

Beau: French for 'handsome', which perhaps implies foppishness. George Bryan Brummell (1778-1840) was nicknamed Beau because of his stylish appearance.

Beaumont: This Old French name means 'from the beautiful mountain' and is a common surname as well as first name.

Ben: Hebrew, meaning 'son', this is a diminutive of Benedict, Benjamin, Benoni.

Joseph Benedict (Ben) Chifley was the son of a blacksmith who overcame social and educational disadvantages to become Prime Minister of Australia in 1945.

Benedict: From Latin meaning 'blessed' and literally 'of the benediction'.

This name spread though the Christian world because of St Benedict of Nursia, born in 480, who established the monastic communities of the Benedictines, makers of the liqueur. Other forms are Ben, Bendix, Benedick, Benedix, Bennett, Benny, Dixon.

Benjamin: Hebrew meaning 'the son of my right hand', this name was given by Jacob to his favourite son, who founded one of the tribes of Israel. A popular name in Puritan England and later America.

Other forms are Ben, Benji, Benjy, Bennie, Benny.

Bernard: Teutonic name which means 'as brave as a bear'.

The St Bernard dog was named after St Bernard of Menton who founded the alpine hospice for travellers in the tenth century. Also Barnard, Barnett, Barney and Bernie.

Bertram: Old High German for 'bright raven', this bird was believed to have great wisdom.

Bevan: Celtic name meaning 'a young archer', this is from the Welsh ap-Evan or son of Evan. Also Bevin.

Blaine: The Anglo-Saxon meaning is 'to bubble or blow', and the Celtic is 'thin, hungry-looking'. In spite of these descriptions, this is a popular name, and there seem to be many un-hungry, bubbling Blaines around. Also Blayne and Blane.

Blair: This strong Celtic name means 'a spot' or 'a place' and literally 'a suitable battle-field'. Like Blaine, this is currently popular and one of the names for tomorrow's surfers and skateboard riders.

Blake: An Anglo-Saxon name meaning 'to bleach', this began as an occupational name for a bleacher of linens.

Boris: Russian, meaning 'a fighter' or 'a warrior' and was chosen by William Pratt for his stage name, Boris Karloff.

Bowen: Celtic for 'descendant of Owen', this is a proud Welsh name which would have originally appeared as ap-Owen, or son of Owen.

Boyce: From the French, meaning 'of the *bois* or woods'.

Boyd: A Celtic name for 'fair-haired', this has become quite popular in recent years.

Braden: An Anglo-Saxon name meaning 'from the broad valley'. Brad, or 'broad' appears in many early English place names.

Bradley: Anglo-Saxon 'from the broad meadow'. The diminutive form is Brad.

Brendan: This Celtic name has been said to have the unfortunate meaning of 'strong-smelling hair'.

A more salubrious explanation is 'dweller by the beacon'. This form gave the Irish surname, Brennan.

Also Brandon and Bredon.

Brent: An Anglo-Saxon name meaning 'the steep', or 'the tall and erect'.

Brett: This Celtic name means 'from Brittany' or 'a Breton'. A very popular name of the 1970s and 80s, and in 1939 given to Australian artist, Brett Whiteley.

Brewster: Teutonic name for a brewer.

Brian: From the Celtic *brigh* meaning 'strength'.

The first recorded bearer of this name is the medieval King Brian Boru, who led his warriors in numerous battles against the Danes driving them out of Ireland in 1014. King Brian's descendants populate the earth as Brians, Bryans, MacBrians and O'Bryans etc. Other forms are Briant, Brien, Bryan and Bryant.

Brice: A Celtic name meaning 'swift or ambitious'.

Brice was a fifth century French saint much revered in medieval Britain. Also Bryce.

Brock: An Old English name which means 'a badger', but to Australians means car-racing, through the hero of many boys, Peter Brock.

Bruce: This Old French name means 'of the brush' or 'of the thicket' and is a place name from Bruis in Normandy.

Scotland's hero, King Robert the Bruce, gave this name popularity in the fourteenth century. Still thriving in Scotland and seen in the United Kingdom as the archetypal male Australian name.

Bruno: A German name meaning 'brown, bear-like'.

Bryce: See Brice.

Byron: Middle English meaning 'from the cottage' or 'cowman'. This name became popular after the English poet Lord Byron.

C

Cain: The Hebrew meaning is 'possessed' and the Irish and Gaelic, 'tribute'. Son of Adam and Eve and murderer of his brother Abel. Other forms are Caine, Kane, Kayne.

Caleb: Hebrew name meaning 'a dog', Caleb of the Bible was the faithful companion who followed Joshua into the Promised Land. Hence this name became a synonym for affection and fidelity. Also Cal.

Calvin: Latin name meaning 'the bald'. Cal for short.

Cameron: Gaelic, meaning 'crooked nose,' this Scottish clan name was adopted as a first name and now is common as both. The short form is Cam.

Campbell: This Gaelic name for 'curved mouth' began as a clan name but is frequently used as a first name now.

Carl: The German form of Charles, 'a man'. Also Carlo, Karl.

Cary: A Celtic name for 'one who lives in a castle'. Also a form of Charles.

Carter: This Old English occupational name meaning maker or driver of carts is more common as a surname, but makes an impressive first name.

Casey: Irish name, acceptable as female or male, meaning 'courageous and brave'.

Cecil: A Latin family name derived from 'blind'. In medieval England, a name given to girls as well as boys.

Cedric: This Anglo-Saxon name means 'bounteous and friendly', and was the name of the legendary founder of Wessex and father of the British royal line.

Chad: An Anglo-Saxon name meaning 'warrior', it originated in the seventh century with St Ceadda, who was noted for his humility.

Chandler: Old French for 'a candle maker', this is

one of the 'occupational' names.

Charles: Old High German name meaning 'man', and one which has been in constant use through the ages, particularly for emperors, kings and rulers.

Charlemagne, or Charles the Great, was the founder of the Holy Roman Empire, in AD 800. Ten French kings and fifteen rulers of Sweden have been named Charles.

Charles was so common a name in the Middle Ages that most historical figures were distinguished by nicknames, for example, Charles the Bold, Charles the Bald, Charles the Lame. Two Stuart kings bore this name and now the Prince of Wales, Charles Philip Arthur George, has kept this name in fashion.

Other forms are Carey, Carl, Carlo, Carlos, Cary, Charl, Charley, Charlie, Chuck, Karl. The written abbreviation is Chas, and the indigenous Australian abbreviation is Chilla!

Charlton: Old French/German name meaning 'of the Charles' or man's farm'. Also Carleton, Carlton.

Chester: This Latin name means 'from the fortified camp'. Also Ches and Chet.

Christian: Latin for 'believer in Christ, a Christian', this name was made popular by the hero of John Bunyan's *Pilgrim's Progress*. Other forms are Chris, Christen, Christien, Krispin, Kristian, Kit.

Christopher: Greek for 'bearer of Christ', this name was used by Christians to imply that they held Christ within their hearts.

According to legend St Christopher, the patron saint of all travellers, carried a child across a river and as he felt the weight increase learned that it was Christ he was carrying; therefore he was carrying the weight of the world. Other forms are Chris, Christie, Kester, Kestor, Kit, Kriss.

Clarence: Latin name meaning 'illustrious or bright'.

Clark: Anglo-Saxon, meaning 'a learned man or cleric'. This was the original name for church scholars who were the only people who could read and write. Also Superman's name when he wears his glasses!

Claude: In Latin 'the lame', which described the Emperor Claudius. Other forms are Claud, Claudie, Claudius.

Clayton: Anglo-Saxon meaning 'dweller in the clay town', this is a place name for clay-pits or clay-beds.

Clement: This Latin name for 'merciful' was the name of one of Paul's disciples and favoured by fourteen popes. Also Clem.

Clifford: Old English place name meaning 'of the cliff ford'. The short form is Cliff.

Clinton: Anglo-Saxon for 'hilltop town', this medieval place name has become popular in recent years and is often used in the short form Clint.

Clive: The meaning is 'cliff'.

'Clive of India', General Robert Clive, inspired the use of his surname as a personal name particularly among the British families living in India.

Australian television is blessed with the

sometimes cynical Clive Robertson!

Colin: French short form of Nicolas, it is also a Celtic independent name meaning 'a cub or young animal'.

Conan: Celtic, meaning 'chiefly and mighty', or 'intelligent', this name is remembered for the seventh-century Irish chieftain, and also Sir Arthur Conan Doyle, creator of Sherlock Holmes.

Connor: A favourite Irish name meaning 'lofty aims', made popular by many heroes of Irish legends.

Conrad: Old High German for 'wise or bold advisor', this name arrived in Britain during the Middle Ages. Also Konrad, Kurt.

Constantine: From the Latin *constantia*, meaning 'perseverance' or 'faithful'. This name spread to Greece and then to England. Often shortened to Con.

Craig: Celtic, meaning 'from the stony hill or crag', this name was popular during the seventies.

Crispin: Latin name meaning 'curly haired'. Crispin and Crispian were third-century shoemakers, and are patron saints of that trade.

Cyrano: Greek for 'of Cyrene' and Latin for 'a warrior', famous for the long-nosed Cyrano de Bergerac created by playwright Edmund Rostand.

Cyril: Greek name meaning 'lord', it became an English favourite after the Reformation, possibly honouring the missionary and intellectual St Cyril. Revived in the earlier part of this century but rarely heard these days.

D

Dale: Anglo-Saxon name used for boys and girls and meaning 'from the dale, or valley'.

Damian: See Damon.

Damon: Greek, meaning 'the tamed or taming'. In Greek legend Damon pledged his life for his friend Pythias and the name has come to mean a true friend. Also Damian, Damien, Damiano.

Daniel: In Hebrew 'God is my judge', honouring one of the great biblical prophets. Daniel emerged unscathed from the lion's den, protected because of his great faith. Also Dan, Danny.

Darcy: Old French for 'from the ark, or stronghold'. Also D'Arcy.

Darius: Persian, meaning 'possessing wealth', this was a great name in ancient Persian and Greek history. Also Darian and Darien.

Darrell: Anglo-Saxon name meaning 'darling' or 'beloved one'. Darling, the original form of Darrell, survives today as a family name, and of course as an endearment. Daryl and Derrell are other forms.

Darren: Gaelic, meaning 'little one'.

David: Hebrew for 'loved' or 'loved by God' this consistently popular name has been borne by many heroes from the biblical King David, who as a shepherd boy slayed Goliath to St David or Dawfydd, the sixth century prince who became patron saint of Wales. The diminutive form of David, Taffy, is used to describe a Welshman. Other Welsh forms are Dafod, Dawfidd, Dewi, Devi, Taffy, Tavid.

Dean: The Anglo-Saxon meaning is 'from the dene or the valley', however the Latin meaning 'chief, or leader', seems to be the original.

The American singer Dino Crocetti, better known as Dean Martin, helped the popularity of this name during the 1960s and 70s.

Dennis: From the Greek god of wine Dionysos. Also a popular name for Christians.

Derek: A derivative of the German Theodoric, meaning 'ruler of the people'. A popular medieval name which was revived this century and popular during the 1920s and 30s. Also Derk, Derrick, Dirk, Rick.

Dermot: Celtic name meaning 'a free man'.

Dermot Brereton is the high-flying hero of the Hawthorn football team. Also Diarmid, Diarmuid, Duibhne.

Desmond: Irish, meaning 'man of South Munster'. Des and Desi are short forms.

Dexter: A Latin name which describes the dexterity of 'right-handed or skilful' men, and obviously refers to a time when right was considered better than left.

Dominic: Latin, meaning 'belonging to the Lord', or 'the day of the Lord'.

The Spanish St Dominic founded the Dominican

Order in 1216. Since the Reformation this has been a name favoured for Catholic boys born on Sunday, the Lord's day. Also Dom, Dominick, Dominique, Domingo.

Donald: A Gaelic name meaning 'prince of the universe' or 'ruler of the world'. The name of six Scottish kings, with Donald I being the first Christian ruler, this has always been a popular name in Scotland as is the Irish equivalent, Donal. Other forms are Donley, Donnall, Donnell, Donny.

Douglas: This Celtic name meaning 'from the dark water' was originally a place name, Dubh Glas. *Dubh* was used for various dark colours and *glas* means 'water'. Doug and Dougie are pet forms. Also Dougal.

Dudley: An Anglo-Saxon place name meaning 'from the lea or meadow'. The short form 'Dud' has a rather negative meaning in this country.

Duncan: A Celtic name which means 'brown warrior'. Duncan, king of Scotland, was murdered by Macbeth and immortalized by Shakespeare.

Dylan: Welsh, meaning 'man of the sea'. This was the name of the legendary hero born of a sea god. It became popular again this century through the poet Dylan Marlais Thomas (1914–53).

E

Earl: Anglo-Saxon name which means 'nobleman' or 'chief'. Also Airlie, Errol.

Edgar: Anglo-Saxon for 'bright spear' or 'lucky spear', this was the name of the first recognised king of England, Edgar the Peaceful, grandson of Alfred the Great.

Edmund: An Anglo-Saxon name which means 'richly guarded' or 'fortunate protector'. St Eadmund, king of East Anglia, was killed by the Danes in 870 and became a saint.

Sir Edmund Barton (1849-1920) was commissioned as first Prime Minister for the Federated Australian States on 1 January 1901.

Edward: An Anglo-Saxon name meaning 'rich guard', and a name carried by several English kings, one of the first being Edward the Confessor, the last Saxon king.

Edward has always been a fashionable name and is noted for being one of the few English names that has spread to many other countries. Eddie, Ned, Teddy and Ed are all popular diminutives. This is the first name of former Australian Prime Minister, Edward Gough Whitlam, born in 1916.

Edwin: Another Anglo-Saxon 'Ed' name, this one meaning 'rich' or 'happy friend'. Edinburgh (Edwin's Burgh) is said to have been named after St

Edwin, the first Christian king of Northumbria.
Eli: This Hebrew name means 'the highest'. A popular Jewish name which came into Christian usage in the seventeenth century. Also Ely.
Elias: Hebrew, meaning 'Jehovah is God' and honours Elias, or Elijah, one of the great prophets who lived nine hundred years before Christ. Eliot and Ellis are more common derivations. Also Elia and Elliott.
Elton: Old English, meaning 'from the old farm', it is a place name adopted late last century, and chosen to replace Reginald by Elton John, in honour of the saxophonist Elton Dean.
Emery: This Teutonic name means 'joint ruler' or 'work king'. The German original Amatrich was given to both sexes until last century. Also Emeric, Emerson (son of Emery) and Emmery.
Emil: This Teutonic name means 'industrious', and was introduced to England by the Huguenots. Also Emile.
Eric: Norse name which means 'ruler' became well known through the Viking, Eric the Red. Also Erick, Erik and Rickie.
Ernest: German, meaning 'earnest', this was an aristocratic name introduced to England by the Hanoverian kings.

Oscar Wilde's play *The Importance of Being Earnest* in 1895 further increased its usage. The short forms are Ernie and Ern.
Errol: In Latin this means 'wanderer', which is also

thought to be the derivation of the German form of Earl. This name became well known through Tasmanian-born Errol Flynn, the handsome Hollywood adventurer whose private life was as eventful as his screen life.

Ethan: A Hebrew name meaning 'steadfast and strong'.

Eugene: A Greek name which means 'well-born', and has a strong royal history in early Scotland and Ireland. Eugene was chosen as a name by four popes. The short form is Gene.

Evan: A favourite Welsh name meaning 'the young', which also appears as Bevan, or ap-Evan, son of Evan. Also Euan, Ewan or Ewen.

Ewen: See Evan.

Ezekial: An old Hebrew name which means 'strength of God' but is rarely used today. The short form is Zeke.

Ezra: Hebrew for 'helper', Ezra was the Biblical hero who led the Jews back from captivity.

F

Fabian: From the Latin family name of the wealthy Fabia family of ancient Rome, who were bean growers. St Fabian was the martyr and Bishop of Rome.

Felix: In Latin 'happy, lucky', this name is also

suitable for a cat which has fallen on its feet!
Fergus: Ancient Celtic name which means 'the best choice'.
Fidel: Latin, meaning 'faithful'.
Forbes: A Scottish name meaning 'man of prosperity, owner of many fields'.

Australian Forbes Carlile was an excellent athlete in rugby union and swimming and is regarded as one of Australia's outstanding Olympic swimming coaches.

Francis: German name for 'the free' which came from the Franks, who boasted that they were the only free people and gave their name to France.

The gentle St Francis of Assisi, who preached a sermon to the birds and became their patron saint, founded the Franciscan Order. This name was adopted in England in the sixteenth century and made famous by Sir Francis Drake. Frank is the short form.

Franklin: Developed in medieval England from Francis, this means 'not in bondage, freeholder'. As with Francis, Frank is the short form.

Fraser: This name came from either the Old English meaning 'curly-haired' or from the Old French meaning 'strawberry'. More familiar to us as a surname through the swimmer, Dawn, the Prime Minister, John Malcolm and the tennis player and coach, Neale Andrew.

Frederick: The Old High German meaning of this name is 'peaceful ruler', and should imply one using diplomacy. However, most of the royal Fredericks have been war-loving, most notably Frederick the Great (1712-86), King of Prussia. He encouraged the introduction of this name to Britain through the Hanoverians.

Boys born on Friday were also named Frederick, for the goddess Freya. The German diminutive is Fritz, the meaning of which is 'peace'. Also Fred, Freddie, Frederic, Fredric, Freddy.

G

Gabriel: Hebrew for 'messenger of God' in honour of the archangel who told Mary of the conception of Jesus. More popular as a girl's name in the feminine variation Gabrielle.

Gareth: A Welsh name meaning 'gentle' which was first used in the sixteenth century. Garth and Gary are other forms.

Garfield: An Anglo-Saxon name meaning 'field of war', a far cry from the lazy, cartoon cat who loves to eat lasagne.

Gary: Diminutive of Gareth, Garfield and Gerald, and through common usage this century, has become an independent name. American actor Gary Cooper (1901–61) changed his name from Frank before his rise to stardom.

Gavin: This is the Scottish form of a medieval Welsh name Gawain, meaning 'white hawk'. According to the tales of the Round Table, Sir Gawain was the nephew of King Arthur. Also Gavan, Gaven.

Gene: See Eugene.

Geoffrey: 'God's divine peace' is the meaning of this Teutonic name which originated as Gaufrid and Godafrid.

Geoffrey Chaucer, the fourteenth-century poet, was one of England's first famous men to bear this name.

Also Godfrey, Jeffery and Jeffrey.

George: Greek for 'tiller of the earth' or 'farmer'.

A Roman army officer, St George, was beheaded for his belief in Christianity in Palestine in AD 303. He became patron saint of England, and the idealised figure of chivalry. George was seldom used until the succession of the four Hanoverian kings of that name, the first in 1714. The name became very popular earlier this century through George V and George VI.

Yorrick is the Danish version, known to us through *Hamlet*, and Yuri is the popular Russian version. Also Georgie, Georgy, Jorge and the Scottish diminutive Geordie.

Gerald: From the Old High German, 'spear wielder'. This ancient 'warrior' name was introduced to England with William the Conqueror. The short form is Gerry.

Gerard: Old High German name from *gairu*, 'spear' and *hardu*, 'hard'. Norman immigrants brought this name to England before the Conquest. Jerrard is a variation and the short form is Gerry or Jerry.

Gerry: See Gerald and Gerard.

Gilbert: From Old High German this name means 'bright will'. Gilbert of the White Hand was an outlaw companion of the legendary Robin Hood.

Giles: St Giles was an Athenian named Aegidius, 'wearer of the *aegis* (goatskin)', and is the patron saint of Edinburgh and of beggars and cripples.

Glen: Celtic meaning 'of the glen or valley', this ancient place name is a popular modern name. Also Glyn.

Glyn: See Glen.

Godfrey: See Geoffrey.

Gordon: Old English, meaning 'from the cornered hill'. It was used only as a surname until General Gordon (of the ancient Scottish clan) was killed in 1885 while defending Khartoum. Gordon was then adopted as a first name in his honour.

Graeme: See Graham.

Graham: A Teutonic name meaning 'from the gray home'. This was originally adopted as a family name by a Scottish clan and became a popular first name in the nineteenth century.

Graham Cyril Kennedy, one of Australian television's live-show pioneers began hosting 'In Melbourne Tonight' in 1957.

Grant: An Old French name meaning 'the great one'

or 'the tall one'. United States General and later President Ulysses Simpson Grant made this surname a popular first name.

Gregory: This Greek name means 'vigilant' or 'watchful'. The first of sixteen popes of this name was St Gregory the Great (540–604), but such a consistently 'popish' name fell out of favour during the Reformation. It was very popular in this country from the late 1940s to the 60s. Other forms are Greg, Gregg, Gregor, Grigor.

Guy: An Old French name meaning 'to guide'. This was a common name in England until the infamous Guy Fawkes tried to blow up James I and parliament in 1603, causing Guy to become most unfashionable. It is currently one of the popular short names in Australia.

H

Hamish: The anglicised form of Sheumais and Seamas which are Gaelic forms of James.

Harold: 'Ruler of the army' is the meaning of this Anglo-Saxon name of kings. The name was introduced to England by Harold the Harefoot, the Danish King of England (1037-1040). His son, Harold II was killed by William the Conqueror in 1066 at the Battle of Hastings. Harry and Hal are short forms.

Harry: Diminutive of Harold and Henry.

Harvey: From the Breton *haerveu*, meaning 'battle worthy'. St Hervé, was a blind bard of the fifth century, and many of his songs are still remembered today. The name was common in England as a surname and only appeared as a first name during the last century.

Hayden: This Anglo-Saxon name means 'from the hedge or valley'.

Heath: Middle English, 'from the heath or heather'.

Henry: Old High German name meaning 'home ruler', Henry was introduced into England around the time of William the Conqueror and then became a popular name for kings and princes. Shakespeare wrote plays around four of the Henry kings, and Henry the VIII, and his six marriages, changed the history of England and the English Church.

Henry is back in favour as a royal name through the second son of the Prince and Princess of Wales. Young Prince Henry will no doubt be called Hal, as have his royal ancestors.

Other forms are Hal, Hamlyn, Hank, Harry and Hendrick. The German usage includes Hagen, Heine, Heinrich, the Italian versions are Enrico, Enzio and Henrici and the popular French is Henri.

Holden: An Anglo-Saxon name meaning 'gracious and loyal'.

Howard: This Anglo-Saxon name began life as a surname and became a personal name only in the

nineteenth century. Probably from the French name Howard, 'worker with a hoe'.
Hugh: From the Old German *hugu* meaning, 'thought or mind'.

Hu Gadarn, 'the Mighty', was a Celtic hero who introduced the Bretons to Britain and taught them agriculture. The French dynasty of the Capets, founded by Hugo Capet in 987 AD ruled until 1328. An alternative spelling of this distinguished name is Hew, and Hughie is the pet form. Hugo is the modern German form.
Humphrey: A Teutonic name which means 'protector of peace'.

I

Ian: This is the Scottish equivalent of John, and Iain is the Gaelic version. See John.
Ignatius: A Latin name meaning 'the fiery or ardent'. The Spanish saint, Ignatius Loyola, first a soldier and then a priest, founded the Jesuits, who spread his name throughout the Christian world.
Inigo: A Welsh form of Ignatius.
Ira: Hebrew, meaning 'a watcher'. One of the musical Gershwin brothers.
Irvin/Irving: An Anglo-Saxon name which was used originally as a surname and means 'friend of the sea'.
Isaac: Is from the Hebrew and means happy. The

Australian Governor-General from 1931-36 was Sir Isaac Isaacs.

Ivan: A Russian form of John.

Ivor: The original Welsh form of 'Ifor', meaning 'lord'. In England, Ivo became a favourite name among the Anglo-Normans but is seldom used today.

Other forms are Ivar, Iver, Ives and the French variation is Yves.

J

Jack: This shortened form of Jacob and diminutive of John, has become so popular it is now considered a name in its own right.

Jackson: Old English for 'Jack's son'.

Jacob: From the Hebrew for 'a supplanter'. Jacob was Isaac's younger son who supplanted his twin brother Esau, tricking him out of his inheritance. He became the founding father of the tribes of Israel.

Other forms are Cobb, Jago, Jake and James.

Jacques: This is the French version of the Hebrew Jacob, 'the supplanter'.

James: Has the same origin as Jacob. Its use as a first name in English was not widespread before James Stuart became King of England in 1603.

James is a popular name throughout the world in its various forms; for example Hamish in the

Scottish Highlands and Jimmy in Glasgow, Seamus in Ireland, Jaime in Spain and Jayme in Portugal.

Popular shorter English versions are Jamie, Jim and Jimmy.

Jared: This Hebrew name which means 'to descend', is a popular boys' name of the 1970s and 80s. Jared was the Hebrew name for the Jordan River.

Jarvis/Jervis: A Teutonic name, meaning 'sharp spear'. In France, Gervaise.

Jason: This Greek name means 'healer' and honours the mythological Jason who found the Golden Fleece and won the love of Medea.

Jeffrey: See Geoffrey.

Jeremy: This Hebrew name which means 'exalted by the Lord' came from Jeremiah, the Old Testament prophet. Other forms are Jerry or Gerry.

Jerome: This means 'the holy name' from the Greek and honours St Jerome (304-84), the greatest of the Latin fathers of the Christian church.

Jesse: 'God's grace' or 'the Lord is', this Hebrew name honours Jesse, father of King David. The American outlaw hero Jesse James (1847-82) made this a popular name in Hollywood westerns.

Jethro: From the Hebrew meaning 'abundance' or 'excellence', this biblical name is again popular.

Joel: Hebrew for 'the Lord is God'. The biblical prophet Joel lived nearly one thousand years before Christ. The Puritans used this name which has never been out of fashion.

John: 'God is gracious' is the meaning of this

Hebrew name which originally appeared as Jochanaan. It has been one of the most consistently popular names and spread throughout twelfth century Britain as a name for Christians because of John the Baptist, and St John the Evangelist. The form John is a compromise between two earlier forms, Johan and Jon.

John appears in many countries. The French is Jean, Welsh is Jon and Jones, the Scottish Jock and Ian. The Irish versions are Eoghan, Eoin, Sean, Seamus, Shane, Shawn and Shamus. The Italian form is Giovanni, Spanish is Juan and the German Hans, Johann and Johannes.

Jonas: A Hebrew name meaning 'the dove', the traditional symbol of peace. Short version is Jon.

Jonathan: A variation of Nathan, which means 'gift of the lord'.

The first recorded Jonathan was the son of King Saul and close friend of David. A popular name after the Reformation, one of the best-known at this time was Jonathan Swift, eighteenth-century Irish satirist and author of *Gulliver's Travels*. Jon, Jono and Jonty are popular short forms.

Jordan: From the Hebrew 'to descend', this name is for the River Jordan which was originally called the Jared. This is a popular boy's name today with the short form Jordie.

Joseph: This Hebrew name means 'increase' or 'addition'.

In the Old Testament, Joseph was the twelfth and

favourite son of Jacob. In the New Testament, Joseph was the husband of Mary, mother of Christ. Short forms are Jo, Joe, Joey.

Joshua: From the Hebrew 'God saves'.
Josh is the popular short form.

Julian: A Latin name meaning 'belonging to Julius', from the ancient family who were older than the city of Rome. The most famous of this family was Caius Julius Caesar, greatest of the five Emperors Julian. He revised the Roman calendar, naming his birth-month July, making Julian a popular name for boys born in that month.

Justin: From the Latin for 'the just', this is a name for one of upright principles and morals. Also Justus, Jocelin and Joslyn.

K

Kane: The Celtic meaning of this name is 'radiant brightness'. Also Kayne.

Karl: See Charles.

Keith: From Old Gaelic for 'wood', this name originally appeared as Keth. At first used in Scotland as a surname, then later as a personal name. The use of Keith has spread far and wide.

Kelvin: Celtic, meaning 'friend of ships', after a Scottish river.

Kenneth: This Scottish name which means 'a chief'

or 'champion', was popularized by the ninth-century hero Kenneth McAlpine. The diminutive is Ken, which also means 'to know' in Scotland.

Kevin: This popular Irish name, originally Caomhghin means 'handsome or kind'. St Kevin founded the Glendalough monastery in the sixth century. Also Kevan, Keven.

Kieren/Kieron: Gaelic, meaning one who is 'small and dark'.

Kim: Famous as Rudyard Kipling's young hero, the name means 'one who rules'.

Kingsley: Old English name for 'from the king's meadow'.

Kirk: Old Norse for 'a church' or 'a place by the church'.

The American actor, Kirk Douglas (father of Michael), changed his name from Yssur Danilovitch Demsky.

Kit: See Christian and Christopher.

L

Lachlan: Celtic in origin and meaning 'the warlike'.
Also Laughlan.

Lance: Originally from the Latin for 'one who serves'.

Lang: Teutonic in origin meaning 'the long' or 'the tall', and the diminutive of Langley.

Lars: An old Etruscan word for a leader, but more likely in use here through the shortened Swedish form of Laurence.

Laurence: The laurel became a symbol of achievement and victory encouraging the popularity of this name which, like most Latin names, was rare in England before 1066.

Lawrence is the alternative spelling, and Larry, Laurie and Lawrie are the common short forms. Lorenzo is the popular Italian and Spanish form.

Lee: From the Anglo-Saxon for 'a meadow' or 'a clearing', this surname was first used as a given name in the nineteenth century.

Leif: Popular Scandinavian name from the Teutonic for 'love'.

Leith: A Celtic name meaning 'wide'.

Len/Lenny: See Leonard.

Leo: Latin for 'the Lion', Leo was popular in early Greece and was borne by saints and emperors, and thirteen popes. Leo is the fifth sign of the zodiac.

Leon: French-Latin name for 'the leonine' or 'lion-like'. Also Lionel and Lyonel.

Leonard: The Old German Leonhard is a compound meaning 'as strong as a lion'.

Made popular by the fame of Leonardo De Vinci in the fifteenth century, the diminutives are Len, Lennie, Lenny.

Leslie: This Scottish name which means 'from the gray stronghold', developed from the surname or place-name, or both. Only in the nineteenth century was Leslie, and the feminine form Lesley, introduced as a first name.

Lester: Anglo-Saxon, meaning 'shining' and also 'a man from Leicester'.

Also Leicester and Les.

Lewis: Old High German for 'famous warrior', this anglicised form of the French Louis was chosen by Lewis Carroll, whose real name was Charles Lutwidge Dodgson.

Liam: Irish version of William. See William.

Lindsay: This Anglo-Saxon name means 'linden tree', and was the family name given to the Scottish Earls of Crawford. Since the 1930s it has been a popular girl's name also, usually with the spelling Lyndsay.

Other forms are Lindsey, Linsay and Linsey.

Lloyd: A Celtic name meaning 'the gray', the English used this name as Floyd.

Louis: French form of the Old High German, Lewis, this name was borne by French kings for eleven centuries.

Luke: From the Latin *lux*, meaning 'light'. St Luke the evangelist, physician and disciple of Christ, was a strong influence in the popularity of this name.

Other forms are Loukas, Lucius, Lucian, Lucien, Lucas and Luca.

M

Magnus: Latin for 'the great'.

Malcolm: This Celtic name means 'worker for St Columb', and was given to followers of St Columb, the sixth-century Scottish missionary.

Manuel: From the Hebrew Emmanuel meaning 'God at our side'.

Mark: Marcus was used by the Romans as a personal and a family name and means 'war-like'.

St Mark the Evangelist became Bishop of Alexandria and made this one of the great saints' names.

Mark Twain, author of the classic *Tom Sawyer* chose this name in preference to Samuel Longhorne Clemens. A favourite name for boys born in the month of Mars. See Martin.

Marshall: Anglo-Saxon for 'the steward', the man who looked after the estate of a nobleman.

Martin: A derivative of the Latin for Mars, god of war. St Martin, the Bishop of Tours, enjoyed great popularity in fourth-century Britain and France and many English churches are dedicated to him. The short form Marty is popular.

Mason: Latin for 'worker in stone'.

Matthew: The original Hebrew Mattathiah means 'gift of the Lord', and was the name of one of Christ's disciples, a tax collector known as Levi before being called from his unpopular profession.

Matt is the pet form and Mathias is a variation.

Maurice: From the Latin name Mauritius meaning 'one from Mauretania', the Morocco of today. The Swiss resort of St Moritz uses the German variation. Morris is the original English form, though the French Maurice is widely accepted today. Maury and Morry are short forms.

Maxwell: Old English, for 'a large well'. Max and Maxie are diminutives.

Melbourne: A name from the Old English meaning 'from the mill stream'.

Michael: Originating from the Hebrew, meaning 'who is like God'. Nine emperors of Constantinople bore the name Michael, as did five Rumanian kings.

The name arrived in England in the twelfth century.

Other forms are Micah, Mike, Mickie and Mick, Michel, Mitch, Mitchell.

Milan: A Latin name meaning 'the lovable'.

Miles: Derived from the Old German 'mill' meaning 'beloved'. The Normans introduced this name to England, and it was popular with the Victorians.

Milton: Old English for 'from the mill town'. This became a popular first name after John Milton (1608–74), who wrote *Paradise Lost*.

Morgan: In the earliest form of Morcant, this is a combination of the Welsh *mawr* 'great', and *can* 'bright', but it is also derived from an older name, Morien, meaning 'sea born'. Now also used as a girl's name in this form and as Morgana.

Murray: A Celtic name meaning 'man of the sea' and traditionally a Scottish favourite.

N

Nathan: The Hebrew word for 'gift', this is a name used in English-speaking countries only since the seventeenth century. The compound form Nathaniel, meaning 'gift of God' (the same as Jonathan) was used before Nathan. Both names are in use again with the short forms Nat, Nate and Nathe.

Neil: An Irish name meaning 'the courageous', or possibly through the French, short for Daniel.

Other forms are Neal, Neale, Neill, Nelson, Niall, Niel and Nigel.

Ned: See Edward.

Neville: From the French *neuville* meaning 'new town'. This name was taken to England by the Normans. Also Nevil, Nevile.

Nicholas: The Greek Nikolaos, compounded of *nike* 'victory', and *laos* 'people', became Nicolaus in Latin. The fourth-century St Nicholas, Bishop of Myra, is the patron saint of schoolboys, sailors and merchants. The German short form of his name, Klaus, gave us Santa Claus.

The pet forms are Nick, Nickie, Nicky and Nico.

Nigel: From the same roots as Neil.
Noel: From the French for 'Christmas'. Other forms are Nowell and Newell.
Norman: Old English, meaning 'northern man', for the Norwegians, not the Normans.

O

Oliver: From the Latin for 'olive tree', the symbol of peace. It has also been traced back to *anleifr,* an ancient Scandinavian combination of 'ancestor' and 'remains', and given to a male child in the hope that family traditions would continue. In Scandinavia, the name became Olaf or Olave.

As Oliver it reached England and is recorded in the Domesday Book as the name of a landholder. Pet forms are Ollie and Nolly.

Oscar: An Anglo-Saxon name from *os* and *gar* meaning 'god's spear'. The Irish-born writer Oscar Wilde (1854-1900) changed his name from Fingal O'Flahertie Wills.

Oswald: Anglo-Saxon for 'gods power'.

Pet names are Os, Ozzie and Ozzy.

Otto: Old German for 'rich'.

Owen: A favourite Welsh name, this originated as Owain, meaning 'well-born'.

P

Patrick: From the Latin Patricius meaning 'nobleman'. St Patrick, who had been baptised Sucat, chose this name at his ordination.

The Irish thought the name of their patron saint too sacred to use until the seventeenth century, but since then it has been one of the most popular boys' names.

Other forms are Padraic, Padrick, Patric, Pat and Paddy.

Paul: In Latin 'the little', this name comes from the Paulian family of Rome. The Apostle St Paul chose this name in place of Saul, and it has always been popular. In Spain this name becomes Pablo, and the Italian form is Paolo.

Percival: Probably French from the Greek god Perseus or 'to cut through the valley'.

Also Percy, Persifal.

Peregrine: From the Latin 'to wander'. Also Perry.

Perry: Anglo-Saxon, meaning 'the pear tree', this name is also a form of Peter and Peregrine.

Peter: From the Greek *petros* 'rock', the biblical Peter became the first Bishop of Rome. None of his successors has presumed to take his name, and there is an ancient saying that if there is a Peter II he will be the last Pope.

Introduced to England by the Normans, Peter was

a common name until Henry VIII broke with the Pope. It is believed that J. M. Barrie's *Peter Pan* helped to popularise this name again. Other forms are Perren, Perry, Pete, Pierce and Piers.

Philip: Greek for *'lover of horses'*, and a name of the ancient Macedonian kings who were great horsemen. Philip of Macedon, father of Alexander the Great, colonised the Far East and the name was used widely in early Europe in his honor.

Several French and Spanish kings bore this name, and the Philippine Islands were named for King Philip II of Spain.

Q

Quentin: In Latin 'the fifth' from *quintus*, a name suitable for a fifth son. Brought to Great Britain with the Normans, there is a Quentin in the Domesday Book. Sir Walter Scott's novel *Quentin Durward* (1823) helped to rekindle the popularity of Quentin in England.

R

Ralph: In Old Norse Rathulfr, and in Anglo-Saxon, Raedwulf, this name means 'counsel-wolf'. The name was used for many centuries as Raffe, Rauf and Rafe, and the 'l' did not appear until the seventeenth century when Ralph was adopted.

Other forms are Rafe, Ral, Ralf, Rolf, and Rolfe.

Randolph: Popular as Randal in the Middle Ages, this Anglo-Saxon name means 'wolf's shield'.

Sir Winston Churchill's father, and his son, were christened Randolph.

Raymond: Old German for 'wise protection', this was a knight's name borne by medieval warriors and crusaders.

Rex: Latin for 'leader' or king and the male form of Regina, first used as a personal name in the last century.

Reuben: Hebrew for 'behold a son', this name was popular in early America. The biblical Reuben was the founder of one of the twelve tribes of Israel.

Also Ruben and Rube.

Rhys: Welsh, meaning 'rash impetuous man', this name also appears as Reece or Rhett.

Richard: In Old High German the meaning is 'the rich and hard'. Introduced to England by the Normans and popular for saints, kings and bishops.

King Richard the Lion Heart led the English

Crusade to the Holy Land.

The Welsh form is Rhisiart, or Rhicert, and the diminutives are Dick, Dicken, Dickie, Dickon, Hick, Rich, Rick and Ritch.

Robert: From the Old High German Hrodebert meaning 'bright fame'. This name spread among the Normans before the Conquest and became popular in England and Scotland after 1066.

Other forms are Bert, Bertie, Bobby, Nob, Nobby, Nod, Noddy, Rob, Robertus, Robin, Rod and Rupert.

Robin: See Robert.

Roderick: Old High German name meaning 'famous ruler', and very popular in Scotland. Broderick developed from the Welsh as ap-Roderick, son of Roderick. Rod and Roddy are pet forms.

Rodney: The Teutonic meaning is 'the famed' and the Anglo-Saxon is 'a road tender'. This name became popular in England after Admiral George Brydges (1719-92), a naval hero, who became the first Baron Rodney. Short forms are Rod and Roddy.

Roger: Hrothgar was the original name used by Anglo-Saxons before reaching England, and was replaced by Roger after the Norman Invasion. *Hroth* means 'fame' and *gar* means 'spear'.

Roland: Old German name meaning 'famous in the land', and introduced to England by the Normans. Roland was one of Charlemagne's knights and a hero of medieval romances. Other forms are Orlando, Rollan and Rowland.

Ronald: Scottish equivalent of Reginald meaning 'strong ruler', this was a Victorian favorite.
Rory: A Celtic name which means 'the ruddy'. An ancient Irish hero, Rory O'More, had red cheeks.
Rowan: Anglicised form of the Welsh girl's name, Rhonwen, meaning 'fair and slender', and a form of the Gaelic Ruairidh, meaning red.
Russell: Latin for 'the rusty haired', after the red fox which in early England was known as 'russel'. Rusty, the diminutive form, is a throwback to the meaning.

S

Samson: From the Hebrew meaning 'sun's man'. The biblical Samson was a strong man who became weak when his hair was shorn by Delilah. Samson became a synonym for 'strong man'. The short form, Sam, is a popular name today, but we rarely hear Samson. Other forms are Sampson, Shim, Simpkin, Simpson.
Samuel: Hebrew for 'heard by God'. The mother of Samuel believed her prayers had been heard when he was born. Samuel became the first prophet of Israel and was considered to be so wise that his name has become a synonym for 'a judge'. This has been a popular boy's name since the 1970s. Other forms are Sam, Sammy, Sammel, Sem, Shem.
Sandy: A diminutive of Alexander.

Saul: Hebrew, meaning 'the longed for', this biblical name honours the first king of Israel.

Scott: Old English name meaning 'a Scotsman', for the Gaelic-speaking people of Ireland who moved to Scotland. A very popular name since the mid-1970s.

Seamus: See James.

Sean: The Irish John, which becomes the English Shaun, and Shane in America. See John.

Sebastian: In Latin 'the reverenced one', and name of the Roman saint who was an officer of the guards. When his Christianity was discovered he was put to death by archers. This name is again becoming popular, and the short forms are Seb and Steb.

Seth: This is Hebrew in origin and means 'the appointed'. It was the name of Adam and Eve's third son, who was the founder of the Sethite tribe.

Shane: Masculine or feminine. See John.

Simon: This is the Greek word for the Hebrew Simeon meaning 'to hear'. This biblical name became a favourite in twelfth-century England but went out of favour after the Reformation when England broke away from the Church in Rome. Again a popular name with the accepted short forms Si and Sim.

Sinclair: English contraction of the French name St Clair which means 'shining light'.

Solomon: Hebrew name meaning 'wise and peaceful'.

Spencer: From the Old French for 'dispenser of provisions, or storekeeper'. Originally a surname it

was adopted as a first name last century.
Stanley: Old English, 'from the stony meadow', this name was popular at the turn of this century because of twice-elected British Prime Minister Stanley Baldwin.
Stephen: From the Greek meaning 'crown' or 'garland'. The Normans introduced this name to England and its popularity increased greatly through the English King Stephen (1097-1154), grandson of William the Conqueror. Also Steffen, Steve, Steven.
Stewart: Anglo-Saxon name for 'a steward or tender of the estate'. An old Scottish clan name, and in the form of Stuart, a royal English line.

T

Taffy: Welsh form of David. See David.
Ted/Teddy: Diminutive of Edward and Theodore.
Terence: From the Latin Terentius. Popular in Ireland, and in Australia in the first half of this century but rarely seen in the birth notices today. Terry is the pet form.
Theobald: From the Old German Theudobald,. *Theuda* 'people' and *bald* 'bold'.
Theodore: From the Greek *Theodoros* 'God's gift'. First used as a baptismal name in early Christian Greece after St Theodore, the Greek soldier who became the patron saint of Venice.

Thomas: From the Aramaic, meaning 'a twin', this name is recorded in the Domesday Book. Thomas à Becket, the Archbishop of Canterbury, was murdered in his own cathedral in the twelfth century, and this created a popularity for the name which has never waned. The diminutive is Tom or Tommy and other forms are Tammany, Tammen, Tomas, and Tomaso.

Timothy: This Greek name means 'fearing God' and was familiar four hundred years before Christ after Timotheus, the musician of Alexander the Great. Also Timmy and Tim.

Toby: Short form of Tobias, Hebrew for 'God is good'. A medieval favourite, this is again a popular name.

Todd: Old English for 'a thicket', and in Latin 'a fox'. This name, along with Scott and Brett, enjoyed a surge of popularity during the 1970s.

Travers: Old French, meaning 'from the crossroads'. The other spelling, Travis, is the more common form.

Travis: See Travers.

Trent: This is a place name for the River Trent in England.

Trevor: English version of the Welsh name Trefor, meaning 'great homestead'.

Tristan: Latin name meaning 'the sorrowing' from *triste* 'sorrow'. This name was made famous by the mythical tragic romance *Tristan and Isolde*.

Tristram: From the Celtic Drystan, meaning 'tumult' or 'din'.

Troy: French for 'from the land of the people with curly hair'. A modern popular name.

U

Uriah: Hebrew name meaning 'the Lord is my light'. In the Bible, Uriah was a Hittite captain whose wife was loved by David. Charles Dickens' cunning villain Uriah Heep in *David Copperfield* has tended to discourage parents from choosing this fine old biblical name.

V

Valentine: From the Latin, 'strong'. St Valentine was martyred on 14 February. The diminutive is Val.

Van/Vance: Van is a Dutch prefix meaning 'from'. In a double derivation, Vance is Van's son or alternatively, from the Anglo-Saxon meaning 'young'.

Vaughan: Celtic, meaning 'little man', this is actually an Irish version of Paul which through common usage has become a separate name.

Vernon: A Latin name which means 'to grow green and flourish'. Symbolic of springtime, this name is given to boys born in spring. Popular earlier this century.

Victor: A Latin word taken over into English without change of meaning. Diminutives are Vic and Vick and the Italian version is Vittorio.

Vincent: Related to Victor, Vincent also means conqueror. It has been made popular by association with St Vincent de Paul.

Also Vincentio, Vincenty, Vinny, Vin.

Vivian: A masculine/feminine name, with Vivien being the preferred spelling for girls. Meaning 'the vital or animated', from the Latin *vivere*.

W

Wallace: Only recently adopted as a first name, this honours the Scottish patriot and hero, William Wallace. It is Old English for 'Welshman' or 'Welshwoman'. Another form is Wallis and both variants can be used for girls or boys.

Walter: From the Old German for 'folk ruler', this name was popular with the Normans who introduced it to England. Although not common today Walter was popular earlier this century, which is why there is always a Wally – or two – at Army reunions.

Wayne: An Old English name for 'wagon-maker' and popular during Australia's post-war population explosion.

Wilbur: This Teutonic name means 'resolute and brilliant'.

Willard: Teutonic name meaning 'strong-willed', or 'determined'.

William: The Old German words *vilja* and *helma* 'will' and 'helmet', are the origin of William. William the Conqueror introduced this name to Britain and until the thirteenth century, William was the commonest recorded English name.

William has been the name of four English kings, and was chosen for the Prince of Wales's first son, William Arthur Philip Louis, born in 1982. Always a popular name in this country especially in the diminutive forms of Bill, Will and Willy.

Winston: An Anglo-Saxon name meaning 'from a friend's estate', this is the name of a small village in Gloucestershire. This name has been used in the Churchill family since 1620 and was given to Sir Winston Leonard Spencer Churchill (1874–1965), twice Prime Minister of Britain.

X

Xavier: An Arabic name meaning 'shining' which was given to honour St Francis Xavier (1506–52), the Spanish missionary and saint. Now often used as a second name.

Y

Yates: An Anglo-Saxon name meaning 'from the gates'. This was possibly the name for a guard at the gates of a walled camp or town. Also Yeats, Gates.

Yves: Meaning 'God's mercy', this is the French form of the Welsh name Ifor, and the English Ivor.

Yoland: Of Greek origin and meaning 'the violet', this is the masculine French form of the feminine Violet or Viola.

Z

Zachary: From the Hebrew for 'God remembered', the name of many biblical men. One Zachariah was the father of John the Baptist. A name often used by the Puritans. Other forms are Zachariah, Zacharias, Zak and Zeke.

FOR THE BEST IN PAPERBACKS, LOOK FOR THE

PENGUIN

Born to Whinge Kerry Cue

From filling the baby's inner ear with mashed pumpkin to clothing teenagers with champagne tastes on a bubblegum budget, *Born to Whinge* is an hilarious celebration of the bizarre job of being a parent.

Best-selling author of *Crooks, Chooks and Bloody Ratbags* and *Hang on to your Horses Doovers*, Kerry Cue has written Australia's funniest and most thoroughly unreliable guide for parents.

FOR THE BEST IN PAPERBACKS, LOOK FOR THE

PENGUIN

Baby Care Book Dr Miriam Stoppard

A practical guide to the first three years
This is the essential guide to caring for and coping with your baby during the first three years of life. It provides straightforward, sensible solutions to the problems which any new parent is likely to face.

A handbook for parents
Hundreds of practical tips on holding, handling, crying, feeding, sleeping, playing ...

A guide to growth
A stage-by-stage guide to your baby's physical, emotional and intellectual development.

A guide to health
An authoritative manual of advice on illness in infants, hygiene, safety, home medicine and first aid.